polymer clay ✳ jewelry

The ULTIMATE GUIDE to MAKING WEARABLE ART EARRINGS

. . . .

Rachael Skidmore

To my sons, Jack and Finn. May you always stay connected to who you are and what you are passionate about. To my husband, Chase, who supported and encouraged me through this process. To the many strong women in my life, after whom I've named several of the earrings in this book.

Brimming with creative inspiration, how-to projects, and useful information to enrich your everyday life, quarto.com is a favorite destination for those pursuing their interests and passions.

Published in 2023 by Walter Foster Publishing, an imprint of The Quarto Group.
100 Cummings Center, Suite 265D, Beverly, MA 01915, USA.
T (978) 282-9590 F (978) 283-2742 **www.quarto.com** • **www.walterfoster.com**

Walter Foster Publishing titles are also available at discount for retail, wholesale, promotional, and bulk purchase. For details, contact the Special Sales Manager by email at specialsales@quarto.com or by mail at The Quarto Group, Attn: Special Sales Manager, 100 Cummings Center, Suite 265D, Beverly, MA 01915, USA.

ISBN: 978-0-7603-8273-8

Digital edition published in 2023
eISBN: 978-0-7603-8274-5

Design and Page Layout: Laura Shaw Design

Printed in China
10 9 8 7 6 5 4 3 2 1

contents

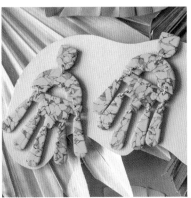

introduction

If you told me four years ago that I would be writing a book on polymer clay, I simply would not have believed you. I started my journey with polymer clay as a side project—a passion project, if you will. I had been the small business owner of a vintage clothing shop for ten years and wanted something creative to do on the side. I have always loved art and expressing myself through creative projects. That's what drew me to vintage—the ability to express myself through fashion in pre-loved, unique clothing.

Polymer clay earrings had a similar pull—something that could provide creative self-expression. It just seemed to fit. I had dabbled in plenty of art forms, from drawing to silversmithing to painting, but when I put my hands on polymer clay, I knew something was different. It felt like I had found something that connected my brain, heart, and hands. It opened a whole new world of possibilities for me.

Polymer clay is accessible, it's easy to use, and the styles are limitless. It is an art form that has been around for decades and one you could study for years and still have so much more to learn. There are countless techniques to observe, with new techniques being thought up every single day.

You're here for a reason—maybe to find a new creative outlet, start a business, or get creative with your kids and make gifts for the holidays. Whatever brought you here, I hope you welcome the journey you are about to begin. You never know where this road may take you.

This book will give you the knowledge you need to dive right in. I am going to share various techniques, some simple and some slightly more complex, that will give you a wonderful foundation for starting your own polymer clay journey. Look for the tips in each project to help enhance your techniques.

Every day I wake up thankful for the opportunities that polymer clay has given me to be creative and to brighten people's day with a pair of colorful earrings or by the knowledge about how to make their own. This is my passion and my obsession, and I am thrilled to be sharing it all with you. Enjoy!

before baking

Polymer Clay Brands

Polymer clay was first developed for dollmaking in Germany in the 1930s. Its usage has grown and evolved over the years, as has its target audience. The first polymer clay brand, FIMO®, is still widely recognized around the world. In the 1960s, Sculpey made its first products. And there was a huge surge in polymer clay makers in the 1980s, which is when polymer clay became more available for at-home users.

Today there are many polymer clay brands available. Here are a few of the top ones you may find.

Sculpey products: A popular clay brand among earring makers, Sculpey comes in a variety of colors in a few different product lines. I'm going to highlight three of the Sculpey polymer clay lines: Soufflé™, Premo™, and Sculpey III®.

- **Sculpey Premo:** Premo comes in more than 50 different shades, including Premo Accents, which showcase glitter, metallic, and gray granite clay among more common shades. Sculpey Premo is a soft clay that is easy to work with, holds its shape well, and is very accessible.

- **Sculpey Soufflé:** Soufflé is a soft polymer clay with a matte finish that is quite flexible after baking. It comes in more than 20 different shades and is one of the more popular lines for earring making. You can mix Sculpey Premo and Sculpey Soufflé to color mix and to get some of the benefits of both lines.

- **Sculpey III:** Sculpey III is readily available at most craft stores and comes in a wide array of colors. However, it can become brittle when used for thinner pieces (i.e., earrings), so it is not ideal for earring-making, as the earrings will likely break over time. It is a wonderful clay for other crafts, though.

Staedtler FIMO: There are multiple product lines within FIMO as well. FIMO's lines include soft, professional, effect, and leather-effect, among others.

- Available in more than 30 colors, FIMO soft is just that—soft. It is easy to condition and mold, and it is very durable and flexible when baked properly. It is compatible with FIMO effect and FIMO professional.

- FIMO professional is a firm clay that takes more effort to condition. However, once it is conditioned, it is a high-quality clay that keeps its shape and is very strong when cured properly in the oven. It comes in more than 30 colors as well and is compatible with FIMO effect, FIMO soft, and FIMO leather-effect.

- FIMO effect comes in more than 30 different colors, including nightglow, metallic, glitter, and neon. Firmer than FIMO soft, it needs to be conditioned accordingly. It is compatible with FIMO soft and FIMO professional.

- FIMO leather-effect is a truly innovative clay line. It comes in 12 colors and is compatible with FIMO soft and FIMO professional. After baking, its surface is similar to leather (hence the name). Thin pieces are bendable, braidable, and sew-able. You can also bake a thin sheet of FIMO leather-effect and cut shapes or fringe after baking.

Cernit®: Popular in Europe and growing in popularity worldwide, Cernit offers more than 60 colors through its many lines of polymer clay, including Cernit Opaline, Translucent, Neon, and Pearl. Cernit is known for having a very clear translucent line, which is ideal for certain polymer clay techniques. It is now also vegan-certified.

Papa's Clay: Papa's Clay is on the firmer side and conditioning may take longer than it does with others, but once conditioned, it is a strong yet flexible clay. It is a great clay for earring-making because it is fairly durable after baking.

Pardo: Made by Viva Decor in Germany, Pardo comes in a wide range of more than 70 different colors of polymer clay and offers reusable packaging. Pardo has several lines, including Pardo Professional, Professional Mica, and Pardo Translucent.

Kato Polyclay™: Kato was developed in 2002 as a collaboration between Donna Kato and Van Aken International specifically for the serious polymer clay artist. Kato is known for its strength and durability. It is a firm clay and will take time to condition. Kato Soft is a new product that will require less time and effort to condition properly. Kato also has a Blackout line that recycles uncured clay scraps and tints them black to help reduce waste. There are many polymer clay brands that have clay softener in liquid form, but Kato is the first to make a clay softener in a bar. This helps revive older clay soften and feel like new.

Craft Smart®: This is the Michaels store in-house line. It's a very soft clay and a bit sticky. It's easy to condition and best for large flat designs, not detail work. Craft Smart has a matte finish when baked.

In addition to these, you may find more polymer clay brands, which are worth checking out and testing. Each clay brand and line has its strengths and weaknesses. Some are better for smooth matte surface. Others are better for caning—having a clay that is hard and holds it shape. There is no "best" when it comes to polymer clay; it really depends on what your needs are. The most important qualities are strength and durability after baking. Everything else is just personal preference for your needs.

Safety

Polymer clay is nontoxic; however, it is not food-safe. When you use a tool for clay, it should not then be used for food, even if it has been run through the dishwasher. Polymer clay contains plasticizer, which can stick onto surfaces and stay there even after washing. Containers, knives, rollers, cutters, and the like should be clay-specific and not used for food preparation after being used on clay. The plasticizer will also stick to your hands, so be sure to wash your hands thoroughly before touching or consuming food. Again, polymer clay is nontoxic, but no long-term studies have been done on the effects of ingesting plasticizers, so it is best not to consume it. Do not use polymer clay, before or after baking it, for food.

When polymer clay is baked, it has a smell. Some clay brands have a stronger smell than others. You may want to bake the polymer clay in a well-ventilated area if you are prone to headaches or sensitive to smells. You can use the oven in your kitchen to bake your polymer clay or you can invest in a tabletop oven. Read more about baking on pages 123-125.

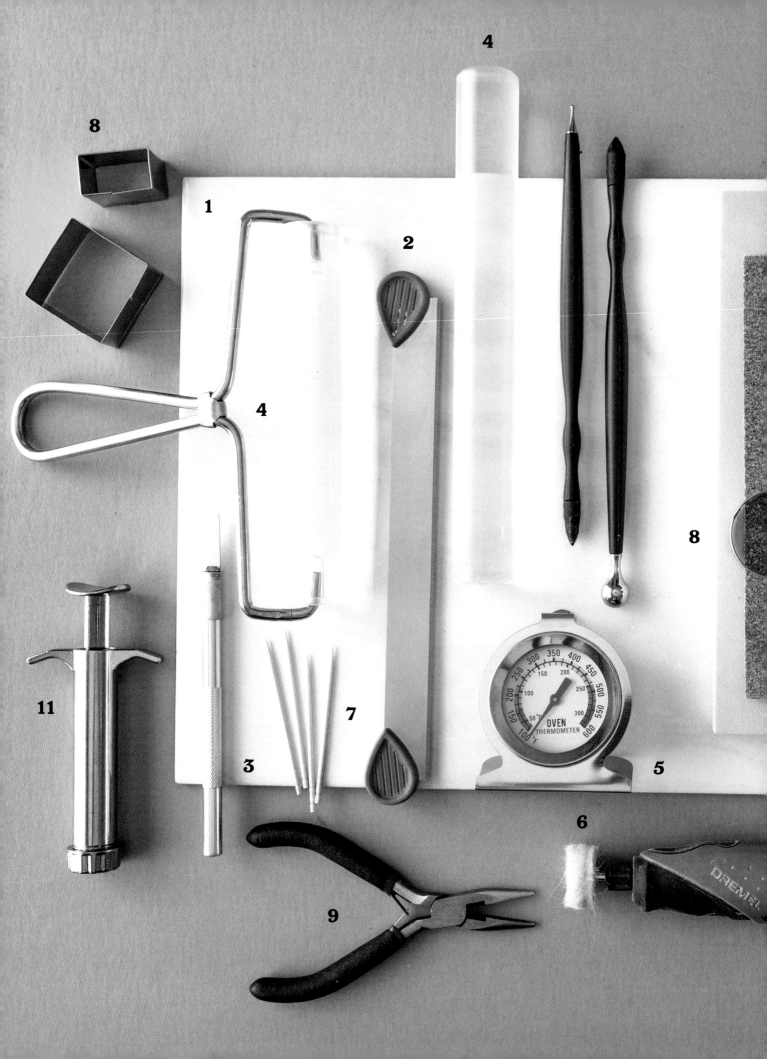

Tools

1. **Tile:** A tile surface is ideal for polymer clay. Look for a smooth, shiny ceramic tile. If the tile has a shiny surface, it will be easier to burnish, or stick, the clay to it. Clay will have a harder time sticking to a dull tile surface. A ceramic tile can also double as your baking surface.

2. **Tissue blade:** This tool will be handy when it comes to chopping and slicing clay, as well as removing raw earring pieces from the tile surface.

3. **Precision knife:** A sharp precision knife will help with, among other things, detail work and removing bubbles from the surface of your clay.

4. **Acrylic roller:** This tool is necessary for achieving flat, smooth clay slabs as well as for conditioning and mixing your clay. You can invest in a pasta roller, but you will still need an acrylic roller.

5. **Oven and oven thermometer:** You can use your kitchen oven or a tabletop oven to bake polymer clay. Polymer clay does not harden, or cure, until it is baked.

6. **Dremel®:** Although a Dremel is not necessary, it is a handy tool for both drilling holes and sanding items. I highly recommend investing in one if you plan to make a lot of earrings.

7. **Toothpicks:** You can use toothpicks to pierce holes in the clay before baking to attach jewelry hardware. You can also use them for detail work if you don't have clay tools accessible.

8. **Cutters:** Although you can use your precision knife to cut shapes, cutters make it a lot easier. You can get creative with just a few circle and square cutters, cutting things in half or using smaller cutters inside of bigger cutters. Or you can invest in a variety of cutter shapes.

9. **Pliers and jewelry findings:** Adding jewelry findings and earring posts is one of the last steps to completing your earrings. We explore this step of the process in depth on pages 116–117.

10. **Clay tools:** Clay tools can be useful in detail work and texturing surfaces.

11. **Extruder:** This tool can be used to make long tubes of clay in various shapes, using the extruder plates. This is helpful for making hoops and caning, and for smaller detail work.

Jewelry Hardware

Jewelry findings are what keep it all together. Whether it's a simple flat back post on a pair of studs, colorful jump rings adding some flair, or fanciful metal findings glamming it up, findings make a piece of jewelry complete. Finding a supplier of jewelry findings is a huge part of the process and one you may need to play around with so you know exactly what works for you in terms of costs and functionality.

When it comes to earring backs, I recommend using surgical-grade titanium posts. They are sturdy, affordable, and hypoallergenic. Individuals who have sensitivities to metal are less likely to have a reaction to titanium alloy posts, as opposed to stainless steel. You can also use sterling silver, though it is a softer metal and bends easier than titanium does. Gold-plated findings are an affordable option that are also hypoallergenic. Gold-plated jewelry is typically brass or stainless steel covered in a thin layer of gold alloy. Gold-filled findings are a step up from gold-plated and can be more expensive but tend to last longer. The layer of gold alloy is thicker than it is on gold-plated findings.

Another option for earring are ones where you do not have to attach a post to the back of clay. You can drill a hole and add a ball post, a French hook, a hoop top, or the like to complete the earring. Each earring top can change the look and feel of a pair of earrings. Play around with your options and get a feel for what you like.

earrings & more

The tools and techniques you'll develop throughout the book can be used to create a plethora of designs. As you develop your skills, I encourage you to put your own spin on things. We all have our own story and our own voice to make things that are unique. I hope each technique is a jumping-off point for you to create something special. Use the lessons in this book to make earrings, necklaces, rings, bracelets, or displays (as shown on page 115). There are endless possibilities when it comes to polymer clay.

Color Palette

Before diving in and picking your color palette, it's important to know what color is. White light is a combination of all color; you cannot see color without light. When light shines on an object, color either bounces back or is absorbed by the object. The color that bounces back is the color we see with our eyes. Black absorbs all light, which is why it is the absence of color. All visible color can be organized by using the color wheel, which is composed of six main hues and six intermediate hues created by combining the main hues (which you can see on the "Color Basics" graphic on page 16).

LET'S GO OVER A FEW PROPERTIES OF COLOR.

Temperature: To keep a color palette cohesive, you can choose colors with the same temperature. If all colors in your color palette either have warm undertones (warm leans red or orange) or cool undertones (cool leans blue or green), it can create cohesiveness. This is not a hard and fast rule, but one that can simplify the process.

Intensity: Intensity is how bright or dull a color is. Think neutral or pastel versus bold bright colors or neon hues.

Value: Value is the lightness or darkness of a color. Color can be lightened by adding white and darkened by adding black.

LET'S GO OVER A FEW TRADITIONAL COLOR PALETTE OPTIONS.

- A monochromatic color palette uses one color in varying light or dark values.

- A triadic color palette uses three equally spaced colors on the color wheel. Triadic schemes are most commonly red, yellow, and blue or green, orange, and violet.

- An analogous color palette uses three or more hues that are next to each other on the color wheel.

- A complementary color palette uses colors that sit directly across from each other on the color wheel. It is usually a combination of blue and orange, red and green, or yellow and violet.

When I'm choosing a color palette, I like to go to a local home-improvement store and look at paint color sample cards. I grab a stack of cards to play around with at home. I also use them to help color match when I start mixing custom colors. For more color palette inspiration, you can look at what colors are in your home or in your wardrobe; this will show you what colors you may be drawn to naturally.

Your color palette can also be influenced by the season, an event or occasion you are creating for, or a mood you are setting with a collection. Color can affect your mood, is associated with different emotions, and can provide symbolism and meaning. For example, red can increase the heart rate and can symbolize passion or love. Blue is more calming and can symbolize honesty and reliability.

color basics

THE COLOR WHEEL

Using color can seem intimidating at first, but when you break it down to a few simple elements, it can add emphasis, impact, and style to your pieces.

All visible color can be organized using the color wheel, which is composed of six main hues (red, orange, yellow, green, blue, violet) and six intermediate hues created by combining the main hues (red-orange, yellow-orange, yellow-green, blue-green, blue-violet, and red-violet).

The result? A continuous spectrum of color!

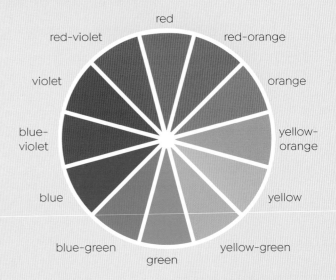

red
red-violet
red-orange
violet
orange
blue-violet
yellow-orange
blue
yellow
blue-green
yellow-green
green

PROPERTIES OF COLOR

All colors are made with three components that can be customized to achieve any look:

value
The lightness or darkness of a color, which can be lightened by adding white and darkened by adding black.

temperature
How warm or cool a color is. Warm colors lean red or orange while cool colors have more undertones of blue or green.

intensity
The brightness or dullness of a color. Think neutral or pastel tones versus bold brights and neon hues.

COLOR PALETTES

Color palettes are formulas we commonly use to arrange or combine colors.

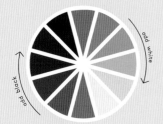

add white
add black

monochromatic
Monochromatic color palettes use one color in varying light or dark values.

triadic
Made using three equally spaced colors on the color wheel, triadic palettes are most commonly red, yellow, and blue or green, orange, and violet.

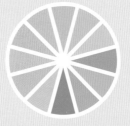

analogous
Analogous color palettes use three or more hues next to each other on the color wheel.

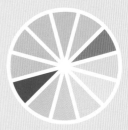

complementary
Made using colors that sit directly across from each other on the color wheel, usually combinations of blue and orange, red and green, and yellow and violet.

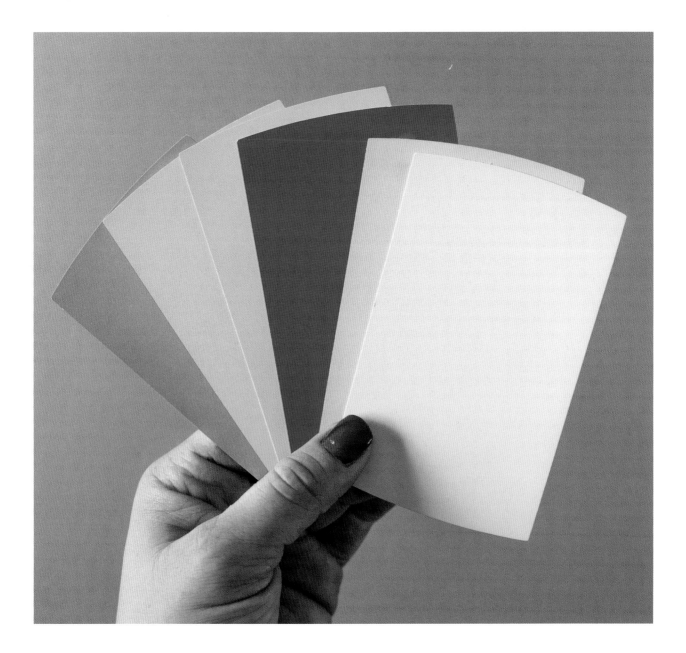

With all of this in mind, it's important to note there really is no "wrong" way to build a color palette. But there is an infinite number of color combinations, so where do you start? This can really depend on a few different things, but I would suggest starting with one. Just one color. What is a color that you are drawn to right now? Starting with one color and building a color palette around it can help simplify things.

After you have picked your initial color, your next color choice will lead you to which type of color palette you are working toward: monochromatic, analogous, monochromatic, or triadic. Use the graphic "How to Pick a Color Palette" on the next page to help guide you.

After you pick your colors, look at them side by side and trust your gut. If something feels off, play around. Look at the color palette in different lighting or pair a few colors within the color palette together and see what combinations you can create within the color scheme you've chosen. Add your magic to it and don't be afraid to break the rules.

What's Your Favorite Color?

HOW TO
pick a color palette

FROM THE COLOR WHEEL

NEUTRAL
black, white, gray

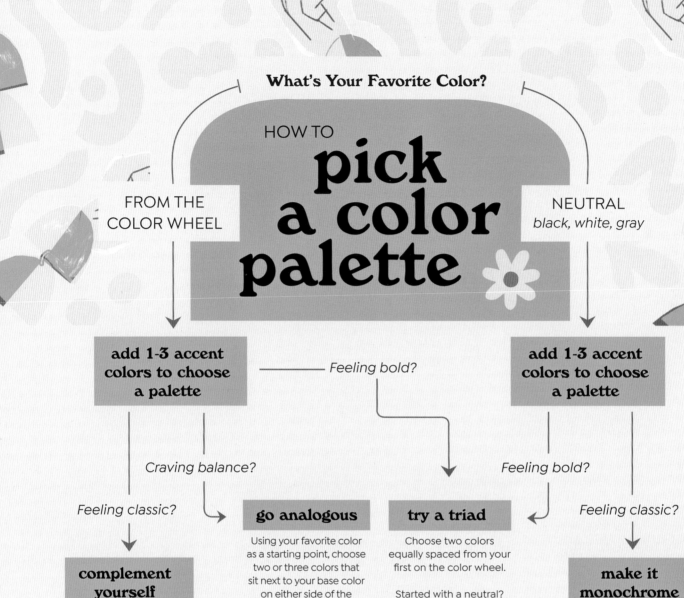

→ **add 1-3 accent colors to choose a palette**

Feeling bold?

add 1-3 accent colors to choose a palette

Craving balance?

Feeling bold?

Feeling classic?

go analogous

Using your favorite color as a starting point, choose two or three colors that sit next to your base color on either side of the color wheel.

Analogous color palettes are a great way to create immediate visual harmony.

try a triad

Choose two colors equally spaced from your first on the color wheel.

Started with a neutral? Pick any two equally spaced colors on the color wheel, and use your neutral as the third member of your triad.

Feeling classic?

complement yourself

A complementary color palette is an easy way to create instant color impact without fuss.

Simply choose the color directly across from your chosen hue on the color wheel, and voilà!

make it monochrome

Monochromatic color palettes are a simple, timeless way to create a big impact.

Simply choose two or three colors that are lighter or darker than your base color in value.

THINGS TO CONSIDER WHEN CHOOSING COLOR

emphasis

What colors do I want to emphasize in my piece?

mood

What mood do I want these colors to convey?

occasion

What occasion am I making these for?

Color Mixing

Creating custom colors is one of my favorite parts of making earrings. Like paint, polymer clay can be mixed to create any color you desire if you use basic color theory. Color mixing is a great way to put your own voice into whatever you are creating. In this book, I use many custom colors in the earring designs. You can find the custom color recipes used in the book within each project.

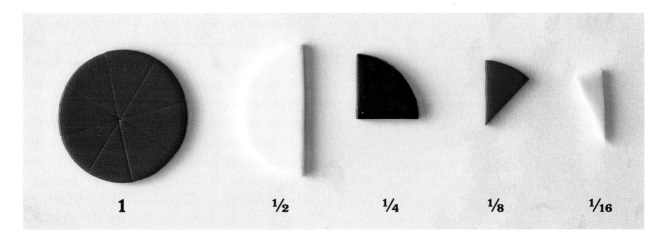

| **1** | **½** | **¼** | **⅛** | **¹⁄₁₆** |

Start playing around with color mixing by starting out small. Scale down to avoid wasting clay while you test out color recipes. Instead of using a whole block of clay to color mix, roll out whatever colors you want to use and cut out circles with a cutter. Cut these circles into equal parts and start experimenting. I recommend cutting them into 1 (full circle), ½, ¼, ⅛, or ¹⁄₁₆ parts. Write down the measurements of each color as you go. If you need larger quantities, you can apply the ratios you develop. For example, one part can equal one block of clay.

HERE ARE THREE COLOR RECIPES.

- **Sage** • ½ part Sculpey Soufflé pistachio and ½ part Sculpey Soufflé bluestone

- **Red-orange** • ¾ parts Sculpey Premo orange and ¼ part Sculpey Premo cadmium red hue

- **Strawberry milk pink** • 1½ parts Sculpey Soufflé igloo, ⅛ part Sculpey Premo fuchsia, and ¹⁄₁₆ part Sculpey Premo zinc yellow hue

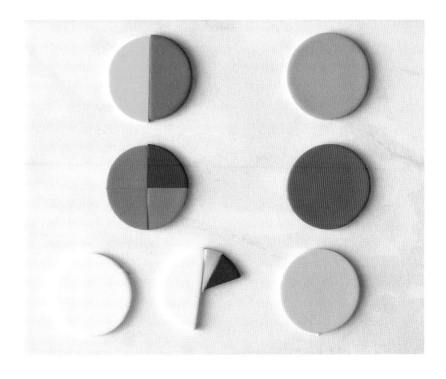

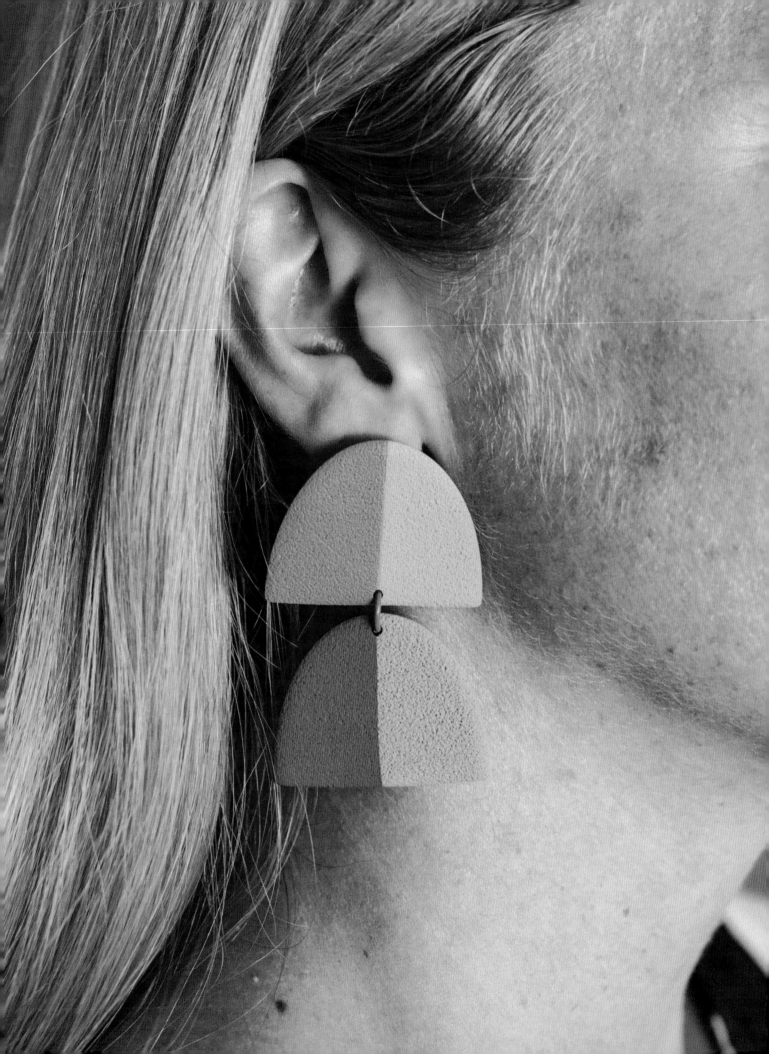

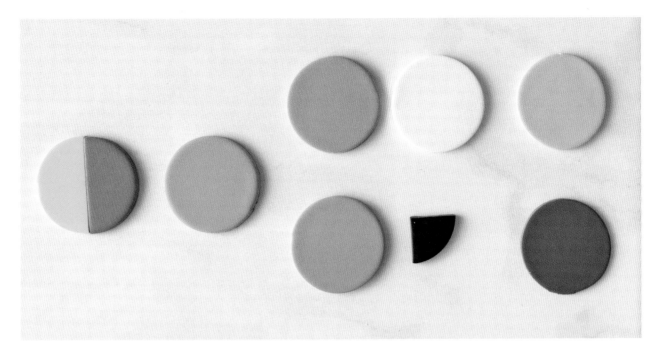

You can also play around with the value of your colors by adding a portion of white or a portion of black. Here is how the color value changes when I add 1 part white to sage and ¼ part black to sage. The white lightens the color value, creating a soft pastel. The black deepens it, creating more of a eucalyptus green.

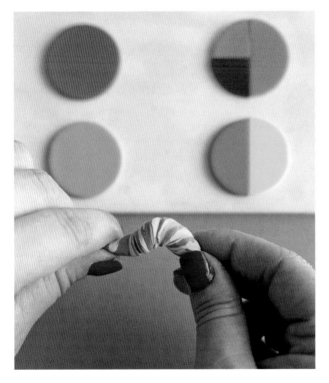 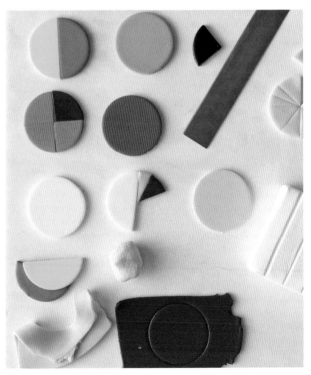

Keeping track of your color recipes helps you to recreate the same colors in the future. Bake a sample of the color you made in any shape you want and use it as a sample. Write the clay recipe on the back of the clay color sample, or number it and write the corresponding number on a notecard with the color recipe.

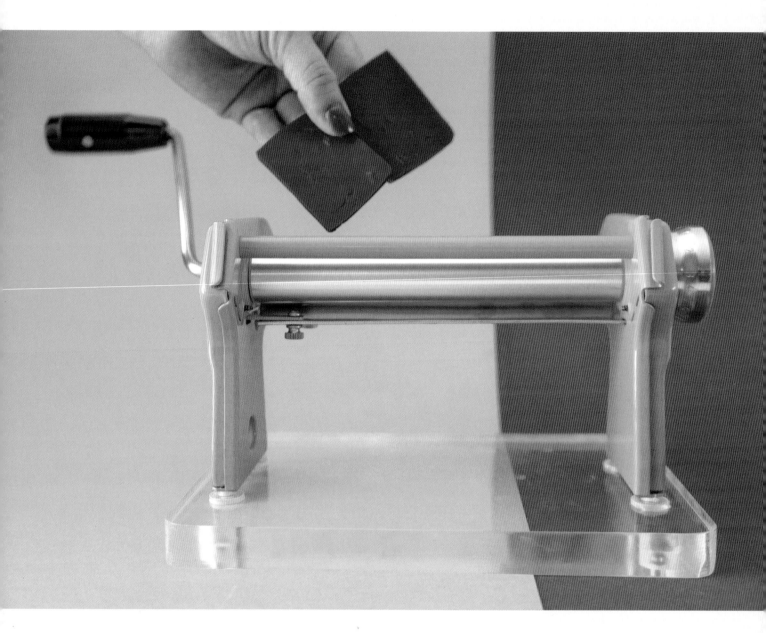

Conditioning Clay

Conditioning clay is the act of "waking up" your clay. It means getting the molecules moving so you can mold and manipulate the clay into whatever your heart desires. This can be achieved a few ways, but ideally you will have access to a clay roller or pasta machine. If you choose to invest in one tool to start out with, let it be a pasta machine.

There are many pasta machines and clay conditioning machines out there on the market today. However, in the clay world, the Marcato Atlas is the most sought after. Made in Italy, it has a reputation for being reliable and substantial. It comes in two different sizes, the 150 and the 180; the 180 is larger in size. You can also purchase a pasta drive motor attachment, as opposed to just using the crank shaft, to make things easier. Although any pasta machine will do the trick when you are first starting out, the Atlas will stand the test of time. You may find yourself buying a new pasta machine rather quickly if you go with a cheaper model.

The pasta machine shown here is a Marcato Atlas that has been modified by Ed's Colors. Ed's Colors customizes Atlas pasta machines to clean the oils and grease off the rollers, powder coats them to the color of your choosing, and adds a clear plexiglass base plate.

Most pasta machines are made for, well, pasta. The only clay machine made specifically for clay is the Lucy clay machine. This is an investment piece made for the serious clay maker. If you plan on working with polymer clay long-term, it may be worth looking into.

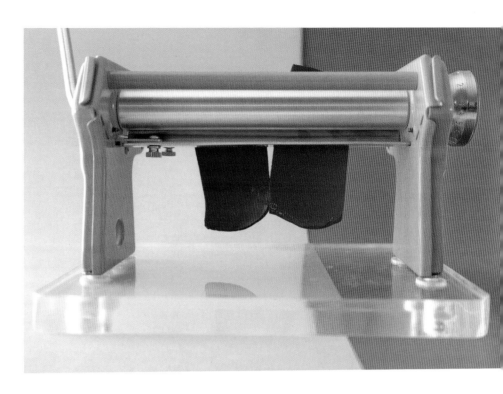

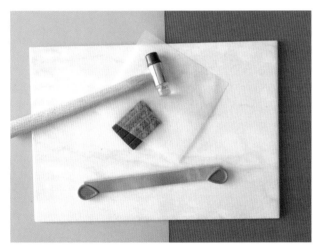

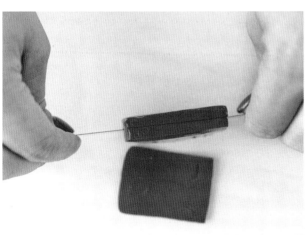

To prep the clay for insertion, cut it with a knife, hammer it flat, or work it flat with your hands and an acrylic roller. Once you have thinned out the clay for the clay conditioning machine, start rolling it through. It may be stiff at first, but as you condition it, it will become softer and more flexible. You will know when the clay is ready to work with when it does not crack when folded.

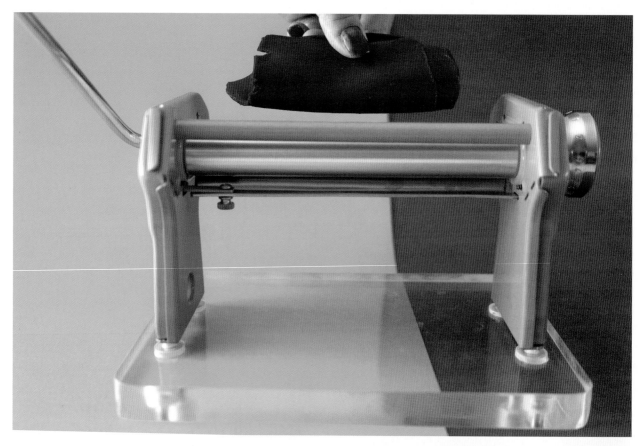

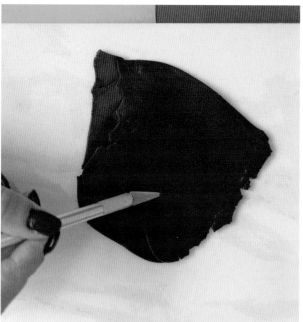

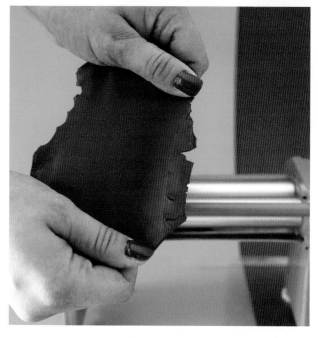

To avoid bubbles, keep the crease, or fold, at the bottom or to the side of the clay. Letting the air travel up and out will help you avoid air pockets in the clay. If bubbles arise, simply pop them with a precision knife. You can also use the "pull method" to remove bubbles in your clay while conditioning it. To do this, stretch the clay and watch the bubbles break open in the clay before folding and inserting into the pasta machine.

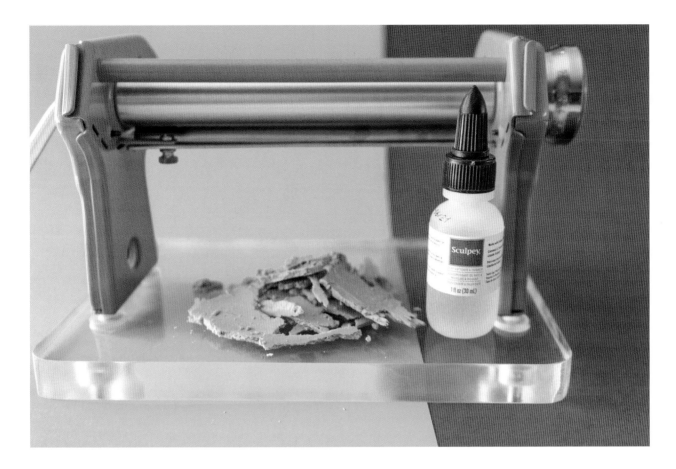

Is your clay too soft? Too crumbly? Some clay brands crumble easier than others. If the clay is older, it can also crumble more easily. Keep working with the clay by using your hands, an acrylic roller, and the pasta machine to condition it. If it does not seem to get better, add some clay softener to the broken-up clay, place it in a zip-top bag for a few hours, and come back to it later.

Some clay brands are softer than others. If your clay is too soft, you can leach some of the plasticizer out of the clay by placing it on computer paper for a few hours. You will notice the paper become discolored as the paper pulls out the extra plasticizer. Once the clay is in a workable condition, remove it from the paper.

If you do not have a clay conditioning machine, you can condition clay with your hands. Use a hammer or an acrylic roller to warm it up. Keep folding and rolling with a clay roller and working it with your hands until it is softer and flexible.

When rolling out a slab for earring making, you can use a pasta roller or an acrylic roller by hand. Typically a slab is between 2 mm and 3 mm thick. It is based on personal preference and design. For a flat surface, when rolling with an acrylic roller, you can use depth guides. These can be purchased in many clay-tool shops. Before purchasing depth guides, I used wooden craft sticks or two acrylic plates as depth guides, one on each side of the clay slab. Roll until your clay surface is even and smooth.

Once your clay is flexible, does not crack when folded, and is as free from bubbles as you can get it, it is ready for jewelry making! I always run an acrylic roller over the clay by hand to remove any ripples from the conditioning machine before I go to work.

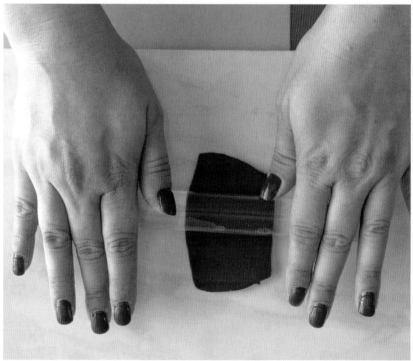

projects

the dua

COLORFUL ABSTRACT EARRINGS

Contrasting colors collide in these fun, abstract earrings. The design provides a canvas on which to show off your custom color palette. Keep it simple with two colors throughout, or go wild and use eight colors like I've done.

clay colors

Lavender: 1 part Sculpey Soufflé igloo, ¼ part Sculpey Soufflé bluestone, and ¼ part Sculpey Premo fuchsia

Fuchsia: 1 part Sculpey Premo fuchsia and ¼ part Sculpey Soufflé igloo

Kelly green: 1 part Sculpey Premo green and ¼ part Sculpey Soufflé igloo

Turquoise: 1 part Sculpey Premo turquoise and ¼ part Sculpey Soufflé igloo

Cobalt blue: 1 part Sculpey Premo cobalt blue and ¼ part Sculpey Soufflé igloo

Tumeric: 1 part Sculpey Premo zinc yellow and ¼ part Sculpey Soufflé latte

Hot pink: 1 part Sculpey Soufflé raspberry and ¼ part Sculpey Soufflé igloo

Orange-red: 1 part Sculpey Premo cadmium red hue and ¼ part Sculpey Premo orange

step 1

Condition the clay colors of your choice. I've used the following color combinations:

° Lavender and fuchsia
° Kelly green and turquoise
° Cobalt blue and chartreuse
° Hot pink and orange-red

step 2

Roll out the clay pieces. Use an acrylic roller or a pasta machine to give each piece a smooth, flat surface. Cut the clay into 2" × 1" rectangles. Lay the rectangles side by side.

step 3

Arrange the clay pieces into a large rectangle with your desired color pairs next to each other. Use an acrylic plate to align one edge of the rectangle and a tissue blade to push the clay pieces until they are side by side. Using these tools keeps the edges straight without ridges or dents caused by your fingers. Push the clay pieces until they are touching without gaps or air pockets.

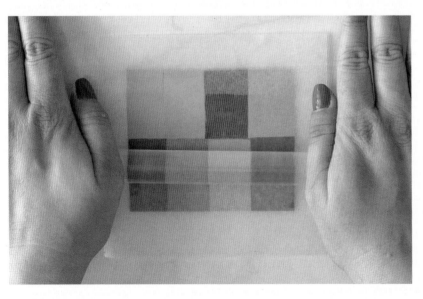

step 4

Use an acrylic roller to make each piece flush and even with the next. Place a piece of wax paper over the clay to keep off dust particles and to create a smooth, clean surface. This also ensures that each clay section adheres to the one next to it.

Pro Tip » Mark your cutters at the halfway point with a permanent marker to help make the color block sides even.

step 5 (optional)

To add texture, place low-grit sandpaper (90 to 150 grit) on top of the clay and roll the back of the sandpaper with an acrylic roller.

step 6

Use a cutter to cut out your desired shapes. Remove the excess clay around the shapes and use a tissue blade to gently remove the unbaked earring pieces from the tile.

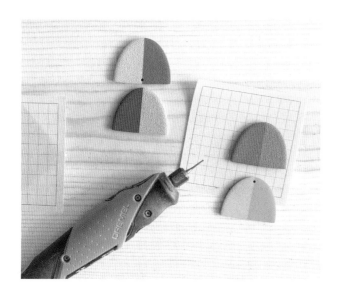

step 7

Bake the clay according to the baking guide on pages 123-125. Then sand and drill each piece.

step 8

Add jump rings and hardware.

the nina

FAUX TURQUOISE

The Nina is named after my great-grandma Martinez, who loved and collected turquoise jewelry. I created this faux turquoise earring in her honor and to complement the turquoise pieces in my own collection. One wonderful quality of polymer clay is how lightweight it is. Although this earring is large, I can wear it all day without it pulling my ears.

clay colors & materials

Sculpey Premo turquoise

Sculpey Soufflé sea glass

Sculpey Premo pale blue

Sculpey Soufflé igloo

Gold foil

Liquitex Heavy Body Acrylic paint in black

TO MAKE THE SHADES OF TURQUOISE:

- 1 part Sculpey Premo turquoise and ¼ part Sculpey Premo pale blue

- 1 part Sculpey Premo turquoise and ¼ part Sculpey Soufflé sea glass

- 1 part Scupley Premo turquoise and ¼ part Sculpey Soufflé igloo

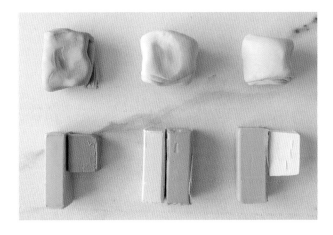

step 1

Select a color palette and condition your clay. I've chosen to go with a traditional turquoise, but you can create this style in any color you want. I've started with a block of Sculpey Premo turquoise. Cut it into quarters and mix a few different shades to add depth. I also used Sculpey Soufflé sea glass and mixed the colors listed here.

step 2

Mold the clay into blocks. Chop the blocks into small geometric chunks that vary in shape and in size from ¼ to ½ inch. The smaller the pieces are, the more veining there will be in the final product.

Optional » Add gold foil. Combine clay pieces and gold foil, if using, in a clear plastic bag.

step 3

Add black acrylic paint to the clay in the bag. Start with just a few drops and mix; you can add more if needed. Make sure all the clay pieces are completely coated in the paint. This is what will create the appearance of veins in the faux turquoise. Add a couple of squirts of translucent liquid clay and mix. The clay chunks should be coated, not drenched.

step 4

With the clay pieces still in the plastic bag, push them into a pressed log. When the pieces are in a cane, take the cane out of the bag. Now it's time to reduce the pressed log. Start in the middle and pinch and squeeze the cane with your fingers to reduce it in size. Press on all sides of the pressed clay with an acrylic plate, working out any air pockets and forming the clay into a rectangle.

step 5

Use a tissue blade to slice the cane into thick, even pieces.

Tip » Using a clay slicer can help with consistency.

step 6

Lay the clay squares next to each other with their sides touching. Use excess clay to fill in any gaps. Then, with an acrylic roller, smooth the clay into a slab with an even surface.

Pro Tip » If the clay is warm, removing pieces from the tile may distort them. Let the clay sit for 20 to 30 minutes to firm up before removing any pieces. If it is a particularly hot day, you can put the clay on the tile in the refrigerator for 15 to 20 minutes to cool it.

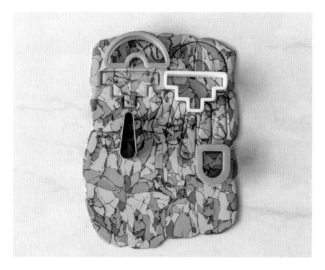

more than just earrings

To use the faux stone technique to make a ring, simply cut the same size circle as the ring surface and gently pat and shape the raw clay into the setting. Bake the raw clay in the ring according to the baking instructions on the clay package. After baking, you can buff the ring to add shine if desired.

step 7

Cut out the shapes with clay cutters. Remove any excess clay. Remove the pieces from the tile. Bake the clay according to the baking guide.

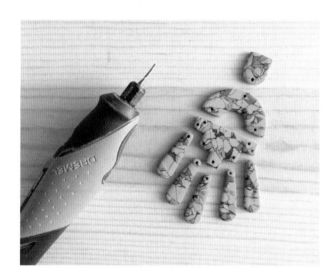

step 8

Once the pieces are baked, sand and drill each one.

step 9

Add hardware and earring backs to complete the earrings.

the marina

LAYERED SLAB

The Marina is an oversized, abstract, mismatched set of earrings that features a surprising, fun display of colors and shapes. This project will show you how to layer clay and how small additions can make a big impact.

clay colors

Soft blue: 1 part Sculpey Soufflé igloo, ¼ part Sculpey Premo cobalt blue, and ⅛ part Sculpey Soufflé poppyseed

Black: Sculpey Soufflé poppyseed

Yellow: Sculpey Soufflé mustard

Cobalt blue: 1 part Sculpey Premo cobalt blue and ¼ part Sculpey Soufflé igloo

step 1
....

Condition the clay. Roll out the soft blue at 3 mm or to the thickest setting of a pasta machine. Roll out the accent colors at the 5 on a pasta machine, about ½ mm in thickness, or as thin as you can with an acrylic roller. Burnish the base color clay to a tile, working out any ridges the pasta machine may have created.

Pro Tip » Pop any bubbles in the clay with a precision knife or needle as you go. Gently smooth over any holes or cuts with your finger, and then smooth with a roller.

step 2

Using a tissue blade and circular cutters, create shapes in your three accent colors. Then layer the accent colors. Starting with the cobalt blue, create long strips and lay them on top of the slab. Roll them from the middle out, working out any bubbles as you go. Repeat with the black and mustard clays. Use circle cutters or a precision knife to cut organic shapes out of each accent color. Arrange them on top of the soft blue clay slab. As you lay them on the slab, try to space them out with the cutter sizes and shapes in mind. Each color should be visible in each earring.

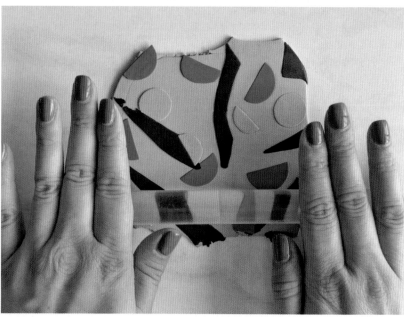

step 3

Gently roll the layered pieces into the clay slab. Hand roll or use a tissue blade to remove the clay slab from the tile and roll it through a pasta machine. Then, once it's flat, burnish it to the tile once again.

Optional » Texture the earrings. (See pages 121–122.) I used low-grit sandpaper and an acrylic roller to texture mine.

step 4

Use circular cutters to create earring shapes in the clay. Use a medium circle cutter and a large cutter to cut two medium circles and one large circle. Remove the excess clay from the tile. Cut the larger circle in half to create semicircles, which makes two medium circles and two semicircles.

step 5

Using a tissue blade, remove the raw clay earrings from the tile to prepare for baking.

Bake the earring pieces according to the baking guide.

step 6

Sand the edges and add posts.

the jenasie

CHECKERED-PRINT EARRINGS

Checkered print is the neutral of the pattern world. Fun and eye-catching, it also goes with almost everything. Use it as an accent or a focal point. Adding a checkered-print pair of earrings to an outfit will instantly elevate it to a more fashion-forward ensemble.

There are several ways to achieve the checkered look, but my favorite is the Sigfus Method created by Lauren Valenzuela of Sigfus Designs. The Sigfus Method offers clean lines, and you can create the checkers in any size you want. Get creative and add multiple colors to achieve gingham or rainbow plaid. Here we'll keep things simple with two colors.

clay colors	
Kelly green: 1 part Sculpey Premo green and ¼ part Sculpey Soufflé igloo	**White:** Sculpey Soufflé igloo

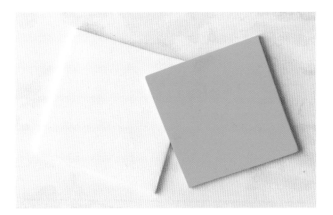

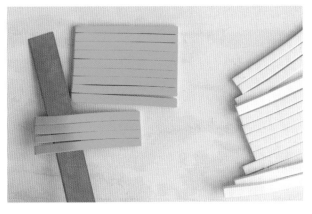

step 1
....

Choose two colors that catch your eye. I've used a vibrant Kelly green and Sculpey Soufflé igloo here. Trim the green and white slabs of clay to the same size. You'll want an even amount of each color to make the checkers. Use a ruler to space your strips evenly.

step 2
....

Starting with one color, use a tissue blade to cut even strips of clay. For evenness, use a ruler to mark each line at the ¼-inch mark. Alternatively, you could use a noodle lattice cutter to mark even lines across the clay.

Remove the strips from the tile.

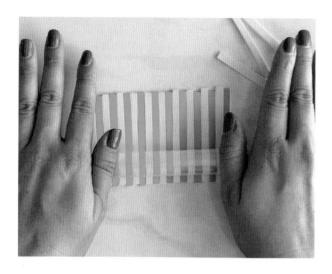

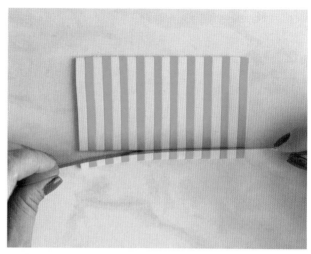

step 3

Repeat step 2 with the second color. Then line the colors up side by side vertically on your tile surface. Use a tissue blade to move them to keep the lines straight. When they are lined up, roll over them gently with an acrylic roller.

step 4

Next, use a ruler to mark even lines horizontally as close to the top and bottom of the slab as possible. Cut off and remove the bottom and top, leaving straight, even lines.

Tip » Alternatively, you can use an index card under wax paper to guide the cutting of your strips.

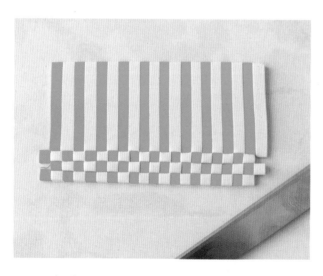

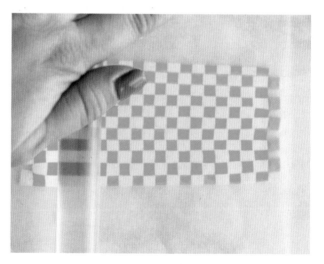

step 5

Cut one strip at a time off the bottom and add it to the top in a crisscross pattern to create the checkers. Repeat the pattern until the whole slab is complete.

step 6

Place a sheet of wax paper on top of the slab and roll over it with an acrylic roller to smooth out the clay. This will also remove any air or gaps between each strip.

step 7 (optional)

Optional: Add texture with a low-grit sandpaper. Lay the sandpaper grit side–down on the slab and use an acrylic roller to roll over it, pressing it into the slab.

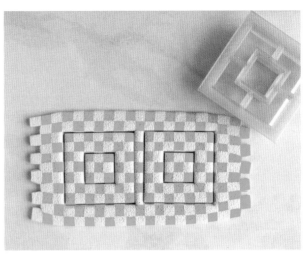

step 8

Use clay cutters to make your desired earring shapes. Here I've used a square cutter from claytimetools.com. Remove the excess clay from around the earring shapes and gently remove the earring pieces from the tile with a tissue blade.

step 9

Bake the earring pieces according to the baking guide. Once the pieces are baked, sand and drill each piece.

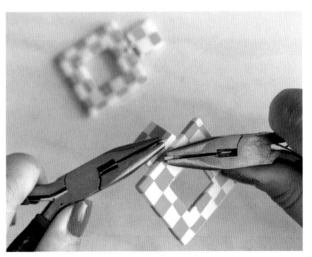

step 10

Add hardware and earring backs to complete the earrings.

the jess

SHAVED TERRAZZO

The Jess is the perfect petite canvas for displaying fun prints. There are several ways to accomplish a terrazzo look, but I like the shredded method because it is a fast and easy way to get the look.

clay colors

Off-white base: Sculpey Soufflé ivory

Tan: Sculpey Soufflé latte

Black: Sculpey Soufflé poppyseed

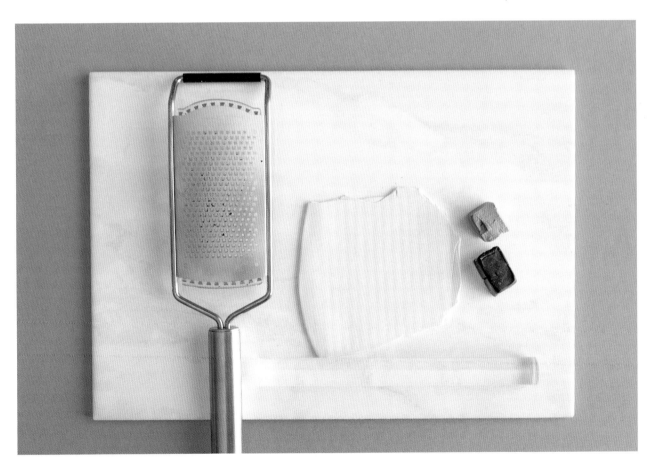

step 1

Select a color palette and condition your clay using an acrylic roller or a pasta machine.

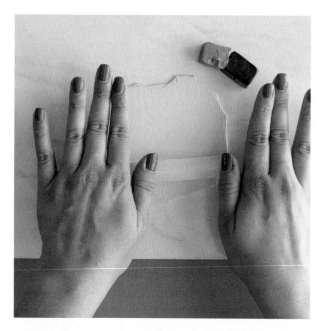

step 2

Lay the ivory clay on a tile. Burnish the clay to the tile with an acrylic roller.

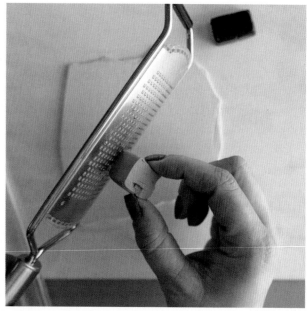

step 3

Use a small food grater to gently grate the tan clay. Let the grated pieces fall onto the ivory clay, spreading them out evenly.

step 4

Repeat step 3 with the black clay.

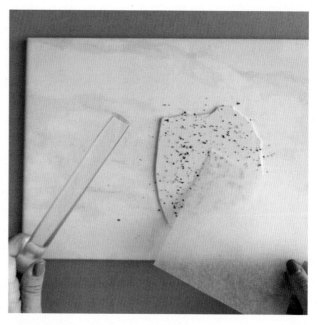

step 5

Lay a piece of wax paper on top of the clay. Roll it with the acrylic roller, pushing the grated pieces into the ivory base. Continue until the clay slab is even and has no ridges.

step 6 (optional)

Add texture by laying low-grit sandpaper over the clay and rolling it with the acrylic roller.

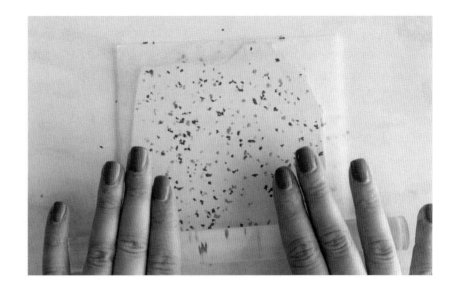

step 7

Cut shapes out of the clay with clay cutters. Remove any excess clay.

step 8

Remove the earring pieces from the tile one at a time. Wrap each piece around a steel straw. When the straw is full, add it to the baking sheet or tile to prep them for the oven.

Bake according to the baking guide. Then sand the edges of each of the earring pieces. Add earring backs to complete the earrings. I used the liquid clay method.

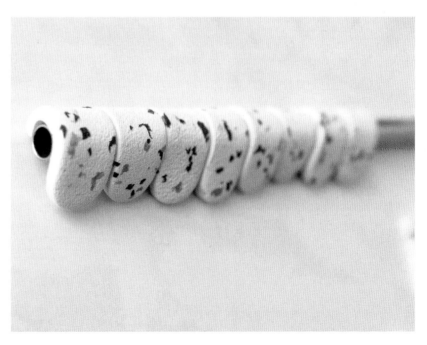

the sam

RAINBOW FLOWERS

Nature is the mother of all inspiration. These flowers blossomed from my love of color and nature. This earring combines a lively color palette and a retro-inspired daisy shape that is sure to pop.

clay colors

Turmeric: 1 part Sculpey Premo zinc and ¼ part Sculpey Soufflé latte

Orange: Sculpey Premo orange

Lavender: 1 part Sculpey Souffle igloo, ¼ part Sculpey Souffle bluestone, and ¼ part Sculpey Premo fuchsia

Soft pink: Sculpey Soufflé French pink

Hot pink: 1 part Sculpey Soufflé igloo and ¼ part Sculpey Soufflé raspberry

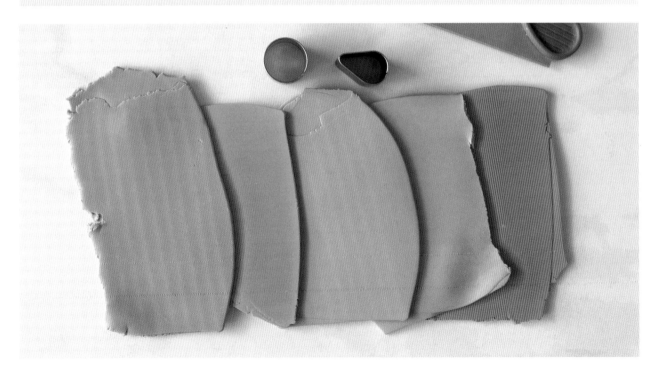

step 1
....

Select a color palette. Condition the clay using an acrylic roller or a pasta machine.

step 2

Lay the clay in petal colors on a tile; then roll it out. Burnish the clay to the tile, working out any ridges created by the clay conditioning machine. Use a teardrop-shaped cutter to cut out two teardrops per color for each earring.

step 3

Cut out a half-inch circle of yellow clay for the middle of each flower.

step 4

Remove the excess clay and lift the earring pieces from the tile with a tissue blade.

step 5

Lay the teardrop pieces side by side to create flower shapes. Roll over the flower shapes with an acrylic roller, making the surface flat and smooth and making sure all sides are touching with no gaps.

step 6

Add a yellow center to the center of each flower. Gently pat the centers into the clay. Roll them with an acrylic roller to make them flat and to adhere them to the clay base. You can use a piece of wax paper or patty paper to protect the clay from dust particles.

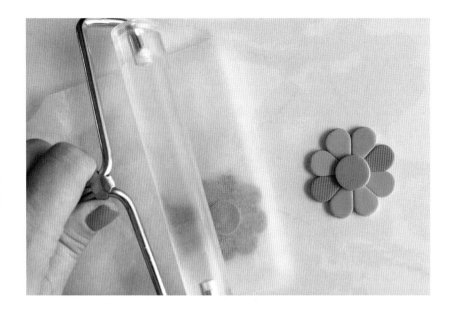

step 7

Bake the clay according to the baking guide. Then sand and drill each piece.

step 8

Add hardware and earring backs to complete the earrings.

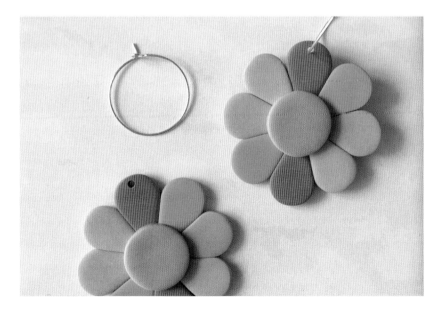

the alex

CLOUDY RAINBOWS

Rainbows bring hope and show the complexity and depth of Mother Nature—after all, you can't have the rainbow without the storm. This earring design captures the storm *and* the rainbow.

clay colors

Turmeric: 1 part Sculpey Premo zinc yellow and ¼ part Sculpey Soufflé latte

Strawberry milk pink: 1½ parts Sculpey Soufflé igloo, ⅛ part Sculpey Premo fuchsia, and 1/16 part Sculpey Premo zinc yellow

Hot pink: 1 part Sculpey Soufflé igloo and ¼ part Sculpey Soufflé raspberry

Pearl: Sculpey Premo pearl

Raindrop blue: 1 part Sculpey Premo pearl and ⅛ part Sculpey Premo cobalt blue

step 1

Select a color palette. I used turmeric, strawberry milk pink, hot pink, pearl, and raindrop blue.

Condition the pearl clay and blue clay with an acrylic roller or a pasta machine.

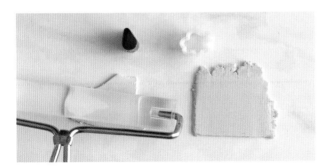

step 2

Roll the pearl clay and the blue clay out on a tile. Burnish them to the tile.

step 3

Use a cloud cutter and a teardrop cutter to cut out two clouds and eight raindrops.

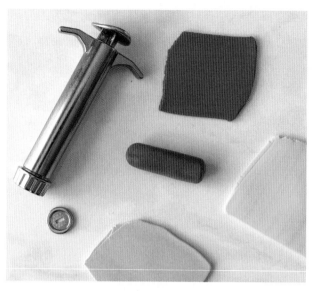

step 4

Remove the excess clay. Lift the earring pieces from the tile with a tissue blade and put them on a baking sheet.

step 5

Condition the yellow, pink, and red clays and shape it for the extruder.

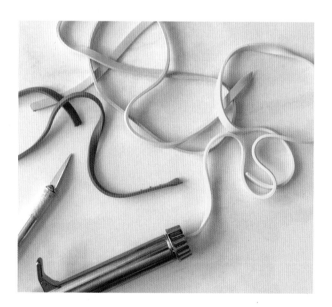

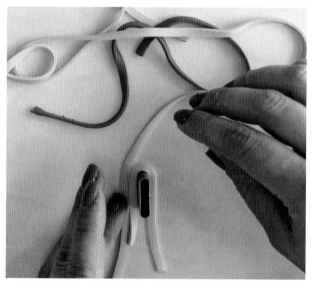

step 6

Use a small rectangle extruder disk to create flat "noodles" in each color. Alternatively, you can use circle disks for a different shape and look.

step 7

Wrap the clay noodles around an oval cutter to make the arch of the rainbow. Lay them around the cutter one at a time, making sure all edges touch with no gaps.

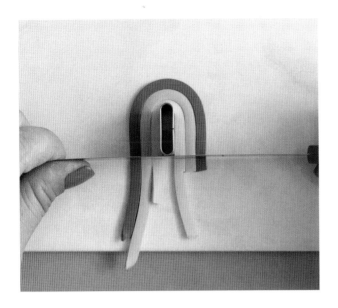

step 8

Gently pat the clay noodles together and cut the ends at the base of the cutter.

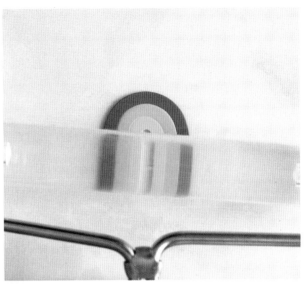

step 9

Roll the rainbow with an acrylic roller to make it flat and to adhere the noodles together.

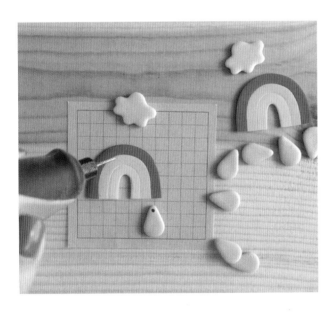

step 10

Use a tissue blade to remove the pieces and prep for baking. Bake the earring pieces according to the baking guide. Sand and drill each piece.

step 11

Add hardware and earring backs to complete the earrings.

the lara

MOKUME-GANE CANE

This traditional Japanese metal technique, Mokume-Gane, was developed hundreds of years ago by Denbei Shoami to look like wood grain. Polymer clay is an ideal medium with which to mimic this traditional technique.

clay colors

Turmeric: 1 part Sculpey Premo zinc yellow and ¼ part Sculpey Soufflé latte

Strawberry milk pink: 1½ parts Sculpey Soufflé igloo, ⅛ part Sculpey Premo fuchsia, and ¹⁄₁₆ part Sculpey Premo zinc yellow

Bright orange: 1 part Sculpey Premo orange and 1 part Sculpey Premo yellow

Orange-red: 1 part Sculpey Premo cadmium red and ¼ part Sculpey Premo orange

Dusty pink: Sculpey Soufflé French pink

Pale blue: 1 part Sculpey Soufflé igloo and ⅛ part Sculpey Premo cobalt blue

Olive green: 1 part Sculpey Premo wasabi and 1 part Sculpey Soufflé khaki green

step 1

Select a color palette. I've used turmeric, bright orange, orange-red, Sculpey Soufflé French pink, strawberry milk pink, pale blue, and olive green. Condition the clay using an acrylic roller or a pasta machine.

step 2

Condition the clay and roll it out. I used the largest setting on my clay roller for each color here. Lay the clay out. Use a large rectangle cutter to cut a rectangle out of each color. Put the excess clay to the side.

step 3

Stack the clay rectangles one on top of the other.

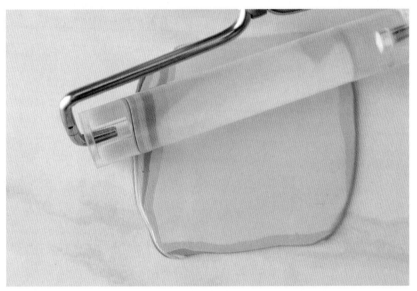

step 4

With an acrylic roller, press the stacked clay down and flatten it until it is about a ¼-inch thick.

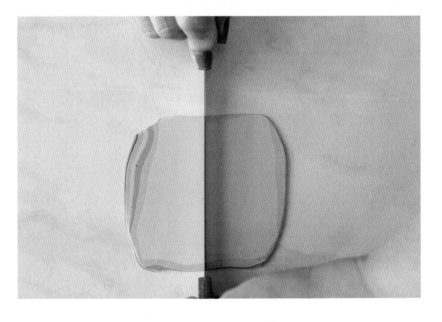

step 5

Cut the clay in half. Stack one half on top of the other and roll it with an acrylic roller. Pop any air bubbles that may come up along the way.

step 6

Using a tissue blade, cutters, and other tools, make shapes and cuts in the clay slab. The more cuts you make, the more intricate the design will be.

step 7

Once the surface is covered with different cuts, start pushing the sides in toward the middle of the slab to make a cube. When the cube is solid enough and won't break at the cuts, remove it from the slab.

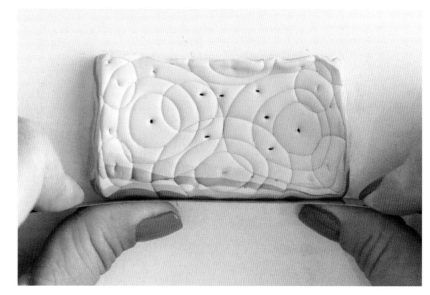

step 8

Use an acrylic plate to press on each side, squeezing out any air and pressing the clay into a firm cube.

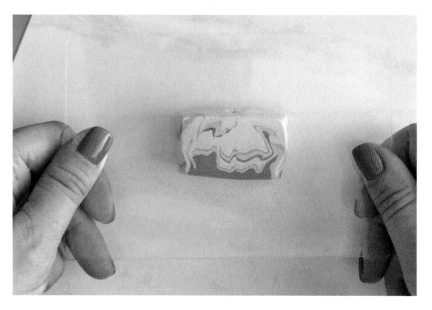

step 9

Slice the cube into equal parts to lay flat and make a new slab.

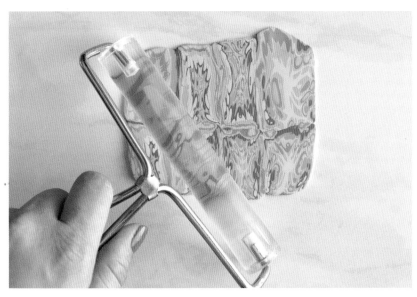

step 10

Lay out the clay slices side by side, edges touching, and roll them into a smooth, flat surface with the acrylic roller.

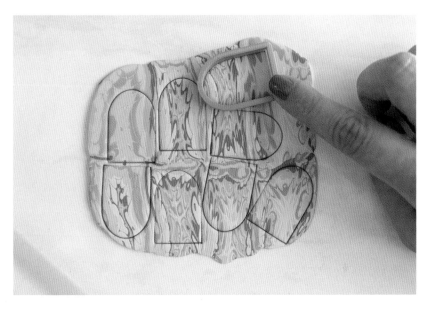

step 11

Use cutters to make your desired earring shapes.

step 12

Remove excess clay from the slab. Using a tissue blade, move the raw clay earring pieces from the tile to your baking surface.

step 13

Bake the earring pieces according to the baking guide, then sand and drill them.

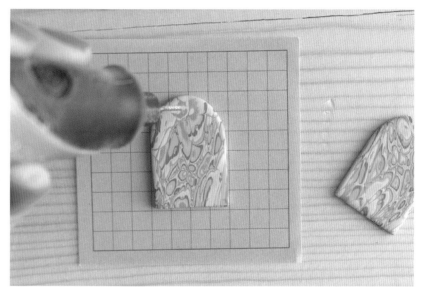

step 14

Add hardware and earring backs to complete the earrings.

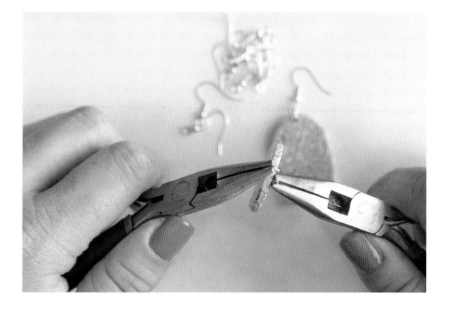

the rae

MARBLE CUTOUT EARRINGS

Marbling is one of the many ways you can utilize scrap clay—a result of every project you do! This project will teach you one method of marbling. You can create earrings from a full marble clay slab or create organic shapes with a precision knife.

clay colors

White base color: Sculpey Soufflé igloo

MARBLING COLORS:

Turmeric: 1 part Sculpey Premo zinc and ¼ part Sculpey Soufflé latte

Tangerine: 1 part Sculpey Soufflé pumpkin and ¼ part Sculpey Premo cadmium yellow

Dusty pink: Sculpey Soufflé French pink

Hot pink: 1 part Sculpey Soufflé igloo and ¼ part Sculpey Soufflé raspberry

Deep sea: 1 part Sculpey Soufflé sea glass and ¼ part Sculpey Soufflé poppy seed

Sage: 1 part Sculpey Soufflé bluestone and 1 part Sculpey Soufflé pistachio

step 1

Select several contrasting colors to marble together. Roll each color into a long, thin snake. The snakes should be of equal sizes. Condition the base-color clay and roll it out into a smooth, flat slab with an acrylic roller or a pasta machine.

step 2

Combine the snakes into one large log. Try to keep air bubbles out. Pop any air bubbles you see with a precision knife as you roll the snake.

step 3

Roll out the log into a long, thin snake. Begin twisting the snake. The more you twist it, the tighter the spirals get.

step 4

Fold the snake in half and continue to twist it together. You can repeat steps 1 through 3 to get finer lines in your marble.

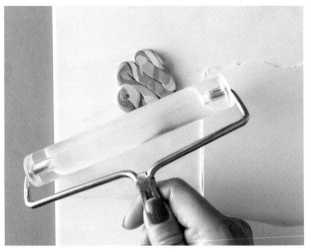

step 5

Once the clay is twisted, push it into a mass, zig-zagging the snake so that the swirls sit next to contrasting colors.

step 6

Using an acrylic roller, evenly flatten the clay into a thin slab. You can run the slab through a pasta machine to make it even and thin. I usually use the widest setting and then slowly thin it to a 4 or 5.

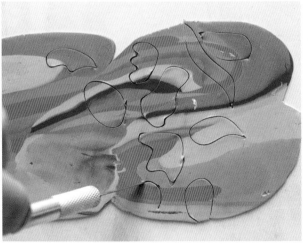

step 7

Burnish the thin slab to the tile surface with your acrylic roller. Use your precision knife to cut out organic shapes varying in sizes. You can make them as big or as small, as straight or curved as you'd like.

step 8

Remove the excess clay from the marbled slab and use a tissue blade to remove each marble shape off the tile and place them on the base slab.

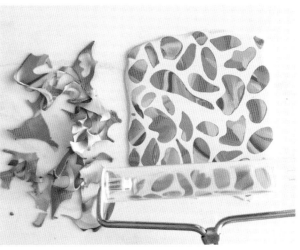

step 9

Once the base slab is covered, use an acrylic roller to flatten the marbled pieces into the clay base.

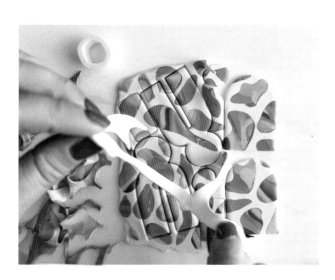

step 10

Use clay cutters to make your desired earring shapes. Remove the excess clay from around the earring shapes. Gently remove the earring pieces from the tile using your tissue blade and add them to your baking sheet.

step 11

Bake the earring pieces according to the baking guide. Then sand and drill each piece. Add hardware and earring backs to complete the earrings.

the mackenzie

RETRO CIRCLES

Polymer clay is incredibly lightweight. These earrings will look and feel like they are floating. Using translucent clay in this retro-inspired earring gives the illusion of bubbles.

clay colors

Translucent: Sculpey Premo translucent

White: Sculpey Soufflé igloo

Pearl: Sculpey Premo pearl

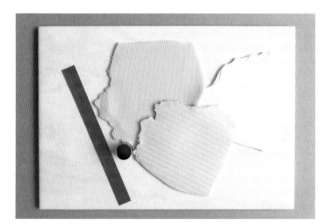

step 1

Start by selecting a color palette. I used Sculpey Premo translucent, Sculpey Soufflé igloo, and Sculpey Premo pearl here for a light and airy feel. Condition and roll out each color of clay. Burnish them on the tile.

step 2

Use a half-inch circle cutter to cut an equal number of circles from each slab.

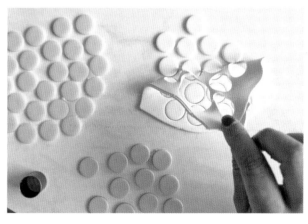

step 3

Remove the excess clay from the tile and set it aside.

step 4

Remove the circles of clay from the tile and stack them on top of each other, rotating each color in a pattern.

step 5

Roll the clay so the edges are smooth and the width is slightly smaller than an extruder. Feed the clay into the extruder. Cut off any excess and save it for later. Repeat with the remaining clay.

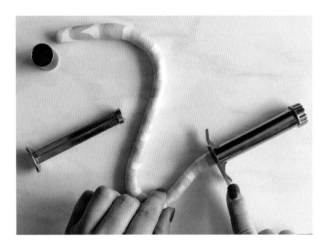

step 6

Feed the clay into the extruder and cut off any remaining clay; save it for later. Then extrude the clay from the extruder and repeat with the remaining clay.

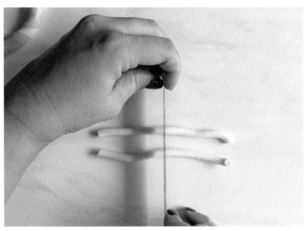

step 7

Line up the extruded pieces on the tile side by side. Cut them in half.

step 8

Line up the pieces and halve them two more times. Once the pieces are cut, line them up in a row of four.

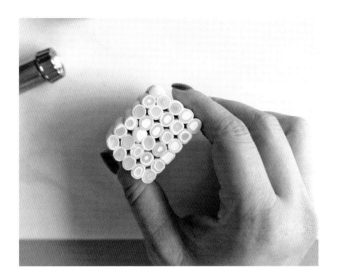

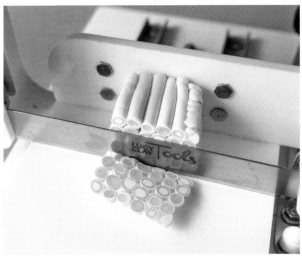

step 9

Extrude and cut any remaining clay and stack them in a cube in four rows of four.

step 10

Slice the cube at a thickness of about 3 mm and lay the pieces side by side to make a slab. Use a tissue blade to cut even slices, or for more precise cuts, use a Lucy Clay slicing tool.

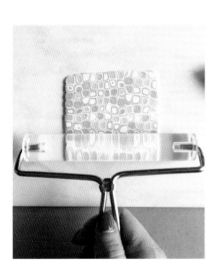

step 11

Roll the slices with an acrylic roller, making a flat, smooth surface with no gaps.

step 12

Use clay cutters to make your desired earring shapes. Remove the excess clay from around the earring shapes and gently remove the earring pieces from the tile with your tissue blade.

step 13

Bake the earring pieces according to the baking guide. Once the pieces are baked, sand and drill each piece. Add hardware and earring backs to complete the earrings.

the saylor

SHELL EARRINGS INLAY

Adding new elements to clay is fun and easy. The small abalone shell pieces in this piece add depth and shine.

clay colors & materials	
Black: Sculpey Soufflé poppyseed	Abalone shell pieces (available for purchase online)

step 1

Condition the clay color of your choice. I used a Sculpey Soufflé poppyseed base, keeping the colors simple here and letting the abalone shells steal the show.

step 2

Roll the clay out to a flat and even surface. Burnish it to the tile surface.

step 3

Gently press earring cutters into the surface of the clay to mark outlines of the shapes you will cut. Do not press them all the way through; just make a light mark.

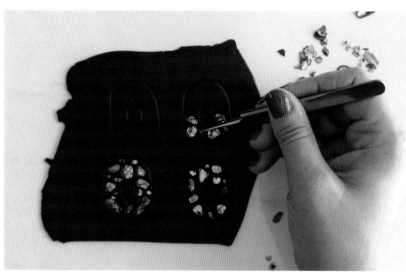

step 4

One by one, press the abalone shell pieces into the clay, about ⅛ inch deep. Using a pair of tweezers makes this easier and helps you avoid fingerprints.

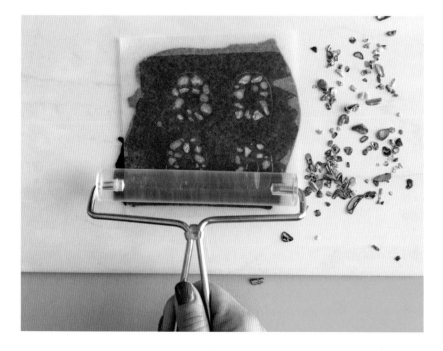

step 5

Once the space is filled with the abalone shell pieces, cover it with a piece of wax paper and roll over the clay with an acrylic roller. The surface should be flat, but the shell pieces should sit in the clay.

Optional » To add texture, use a sheet of sandpaper to cover the slab. Use the acrylic roller to press the sandpaper into the clay, creating a textured surface.

step 6

Use the clay cutters to make your desired earring shapes. Remove the excess clay from around the earring shapes and gently remove the earring pieces from the tile with a tissue blade.

step 7

Bake the earring pieces according to the baking guide. Then sand and drill each piece.

step 8

Add hardware and earring backs to complete the earrings.

the trish

HAMMERED "METAL" EARRINGS

By working on this project, you will learn how to replicate the look of hammered brass. Get the sophisticated look of a metallic earring without the weight.

clay color & materials	
Gold: Sculpey Premo antique gold	Clear sealant
Mica powder	

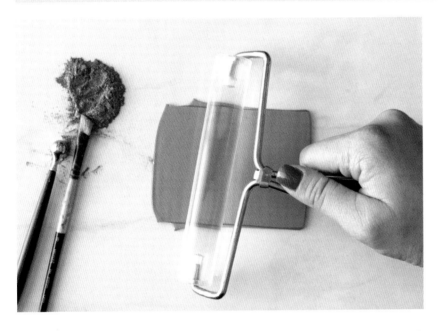

step 1

Select a metallic clay for the base. I've used Sculpey Premo antique gold clay, but Cernit also makes metallic colors. Roll out and condition the clay with an acrylic roller or with a pasta machine. Burnish the conditioned clay to the tile surface with the acrylic roller.

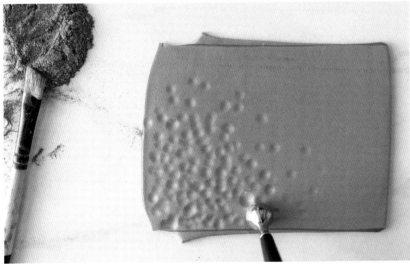

step 2

Use a rounded clay tool to create divots in the clay's surface. If you do not have a clay tool, you can use a rounded pencil eraser or anything else with a small, round surface.

step 3

When the clay is fully covered in divots, use mica powder and a soft-bristled paintbrush to apply a thin coat of metallic mica power to the top.

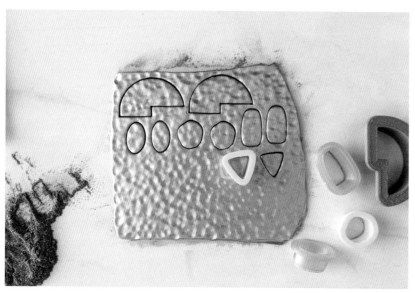

step 4

Use cutters in your desired shape to cut shapes out of the clay.

Tip » Use as much of the clay slab as possible. Make small studs and get creative with smaller, thinner designs.

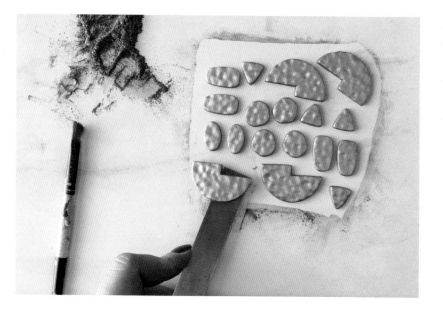

step 5

Remove the excess clay from the slab. Move the earring pieces from the tile with a tissue blade.

step 6

Bake the earring pieces according to the baking guide. Sand the edges of each earring piece.

step 7

When you use powders on polymer clay, it's best to seal it. Mica powder will rub off if not sealed. I used Fimo's clear bead sealant to protect the mica powder. Follow the directions on the packaging for the sealant, and wait 24 hours before moving to the next step.

step 8

Once the sealant has fully dried, drill each piece in preparation for the hardware.

step 9

Add hardware and earring backs to complete the earrings.

the di

BEAD HOOPS

Beadmaking has been around for thousands of years. This simple and timeless style can be made modern with vibrant colors and a wire hoop.

clay colors

Turmeric: 1 part Sculpey Premo zinc and ¼ part Sculpey Soufflé latte

Tangerine: 1 part Sculpey Soufflé pumpkin and ¼ part Sculpey Premo cadmium yellow

Dusty pink: Sculpey Soufflé French pink

Hot pink: 1 part Sculpey Soufflé igloo and ¼ part Sculpey Soufflé poppyseed

Sage: 1 part Sculpey Soufflé bluestone and 1 part Sculpey Soufflé pistachio

Deep sea: 1 part Sculpey Souffle sea glass and ¼ part Sculpey Souffle poppy seed

step 1

Pick a color palette. Condition and roll out each color of clay. Burnish the clay to the tile with an acrylic roller.

step 2

Use a ½-inch circle cutter to cut two circles out of each color. This will allow you to create equal-sized clay beads.

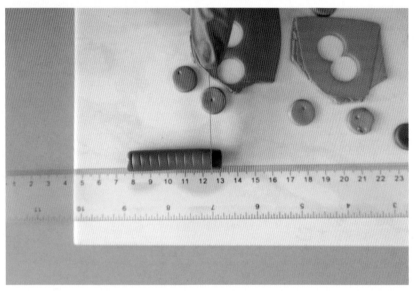

step 3

Alternatively, you can roll the clay into a log and use a ruler to measure out equal parts.

If the clay gets stuck in the cutter, use a clay tool to push it out.

step 4

Remove the excess clay and set it aside. Remove the circle pieces with a tissue blade.

Pro Tip » You can purchase bead rollers that will make beadmaking smoother and easier. Extra beads can be used with other bead designs.

step 5

Roll each circle into a ball with your hands. Wear gloves to avoid getting fingerprints on the beads.

Keep some beads rounded as they are and set them aside.

step 6

Roll the clay beads between an acrylic plate and the tile. This will keep them free of fingerprints and give them smooth, clean surfaces.

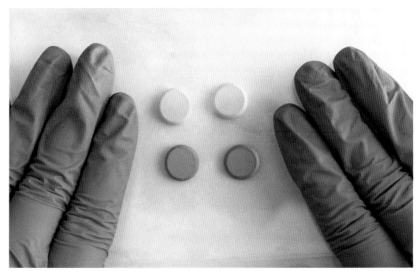

step 7

Place the beads on top of an accordion-pleated piece of card stock. This will help avoid dents or marks in the beads. Put the beads in the refrigerator for 30 minutes to let them set.

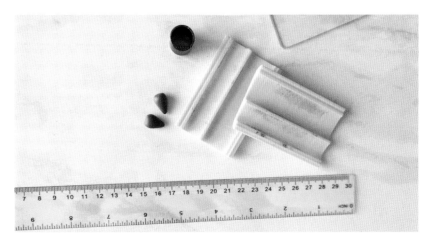

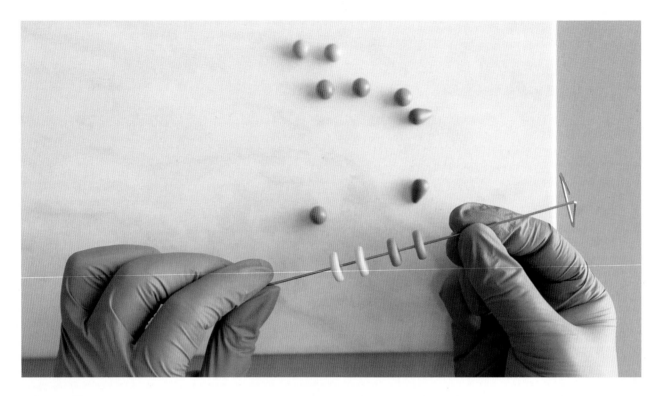

step 8

Using a bead reamer, pierce each bead straight through its center. Twist as you pierce the beads. Leave the beads on the reamer. Alternatively, use a toothpick to pierce the beads.

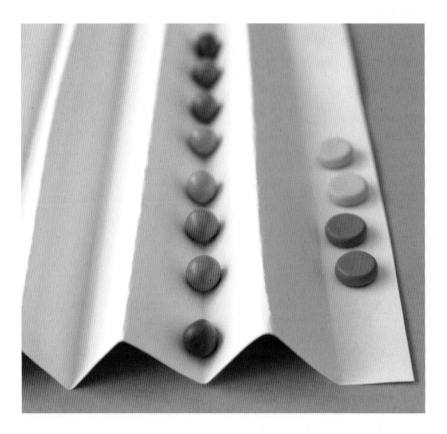

step 9

Place the beads on the baking sheet. If you do not have a bead rack, you can use a piece of paper folded like an accordion like you did for the refrigerator. Due to the low oven temperature used for baking clay, the paper won't burn.

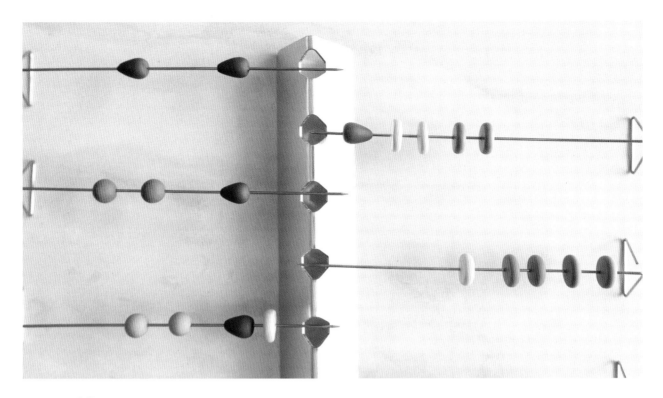

step 10

Bake the earring pieces according to the baking guide. Then sand and drill each piece. Sand any rough surfaces and use a sander to smooth out the holes.

step 11

Add the baked and sanded beads to the flat-head bead pins in your desired configuration. Use a bead looper to create the loop on the bead wire. Add hardware to the wire hoops.

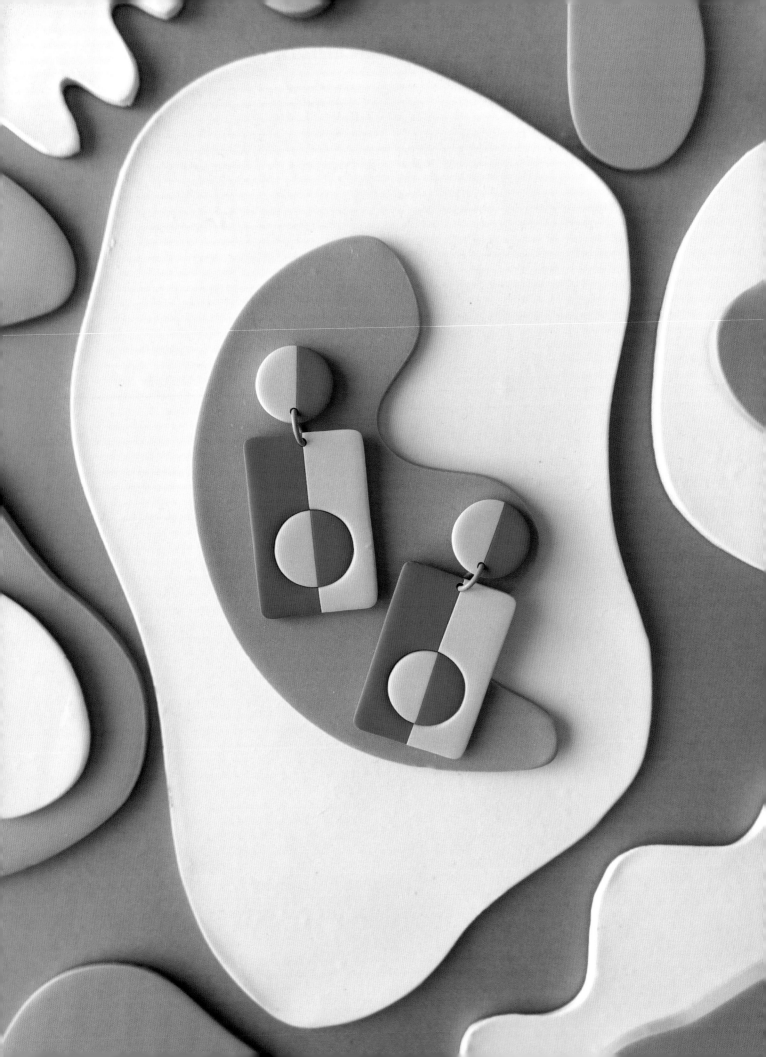

the mj

CUTOUT RETRO

The MJ earring is a nod to the 1960s. Vibrant, contrasting colors give off retro vibes and celebrate the spirit of self-discovery. This earring design features clean lines and modern shapes.

clay colors

Strawberry milk pink: 1½ parts Sculpey Soufflé igloo, ⅛ part Sculpey Premo fuchsia, and 1/16 part Sculpey Premo zinc yellow hue

Cobalt blue: 1 part Sculpey Soufflé cobalt blue and ¼ part Sculpey Soufflé igloo

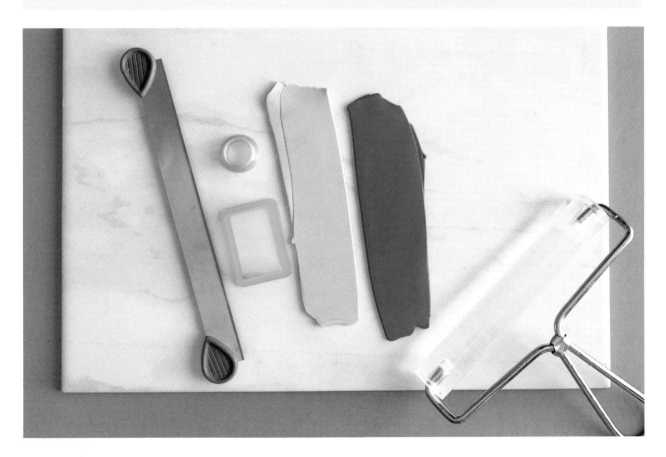

step 1
....

Select two contrasting colors that catch your eye. I used strawberry milk pink and cobalt blue. Condition and roll out the clay using an acrylic roller or a pasta machine.

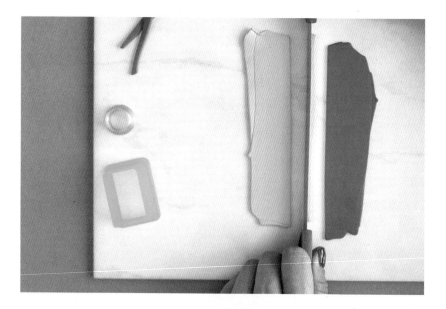

step 2

Make a 1" by 4" strip of clay with straight edges in each color.

step 3

Lay the clay pieces side by side. Using a tissue blade, push the pieces together, making sure the edges are touching with no gaps or air pockets.

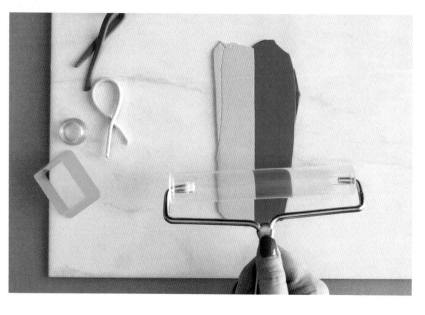

step 4

With an acrylic roller, smooth the surface of the clay.

step 5

Cut out two rectangles, making each color the same size.

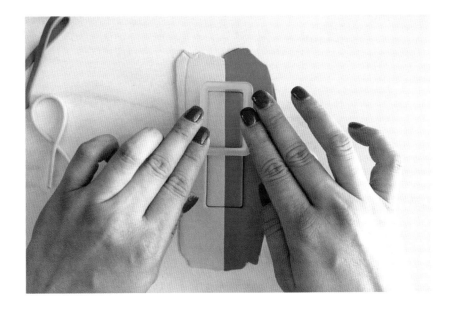

step 6

Use a smaller circular cutter to cut a circle in the center of each rectangle and two for the top pieces—four in total.

step 7

Remove the excess clay and put it aside.

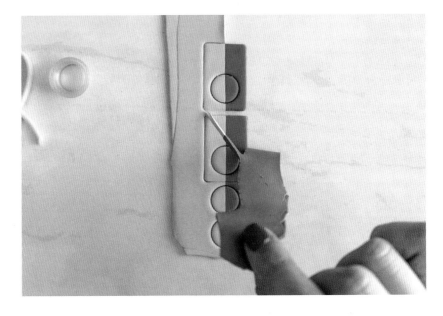

Pro Tip » If the clay is warm and warps when you try to remove it from the tile, put the tile in the refrigerator for 30 minutes to cool down the clay. This will prevent it from being misshapen when you remove it.

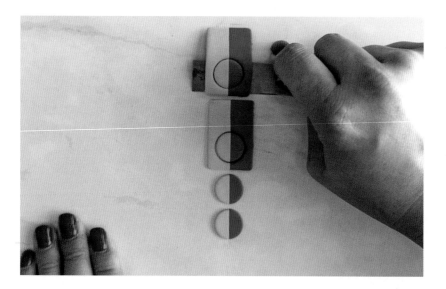

step 8
Remove the earring pieces as a whole, doing your best not to warp them. Gently push the middle circle portion out of each rectangle.

step 9
Place the rectangle portions on the tile again. Turn the circle pieces around so the colors are switched and place each inside the hole it was removed from.

step 10

Use the tissue blade to push the sides in, filling any gaps that may have formed.

step 11

Use the acrylic roller to flatten the surface. Gently remove the earring pieces from the tile with the tissue blade.

Bake the earring pieces according to the baking guide. Then sand and drill each piece. You can use a piece of sandpaper or a Dremel.

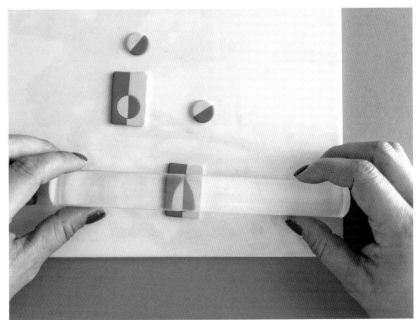

step 12

Add hardware and earring backs to complete the earrings.

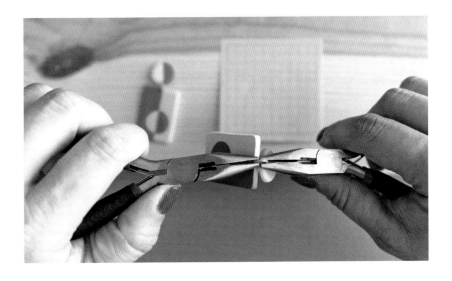

the maggie

TWO-TONE HOOPS

Hoop earrings have been around for thousands of years. Modernize the classic style with this tutorial for colorful two-tone hoops.

clay colors	
Sage green: 1 part Sculpey Soufflé bluestone and 1 part Sculpey Soufflé pistachio	**Deep sea:** 1 part Sculpey Soufflé sea glass and ¼ part Sculpey Soufflé poppy seed

step 1

Select two colors that catch your eye. Condition and soften the clay.

step 2

Roll the base color into a ball with your hands to make sure there are no folds or creases. Once it's a smooth, round ball, roll it into a log.

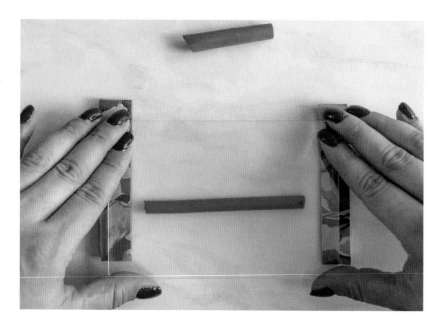

step 3

Using depth guides and an acrylic plate, roll the clay until it is a smooth, even log under the acrylic plate.

Tip » Use excess clay to make depth guides for your hoops. This will help you keep each side level. You can also use two decks of cards (adding or subtracting cards for whatever width you desire).

step 4

Use an acrylic roller to make the accent color into a thin strip. Make it as thin as possible while still maintaining its integrity.

step 5

Cut the accent color into a 1½-inch strip.

Pro Tip » For this project, I will show you how to make evenly sized hoops by hand, but you can also use an extruder to make them.

step 6

Roll the accent color onto the base color. Try to avoid creating any air pockets, which will turn into bubbles after baking.

step 7

Cut the accent color when it is fully wrapped around the base color. Try not to create much overlap. Smooth the accent color over the base color and check once more for bubbles. If there are any bubbles, pierce them with a precision knife and smooth over the clay with your finger.

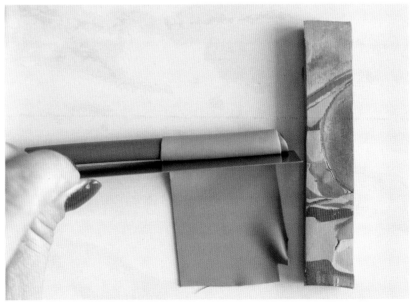

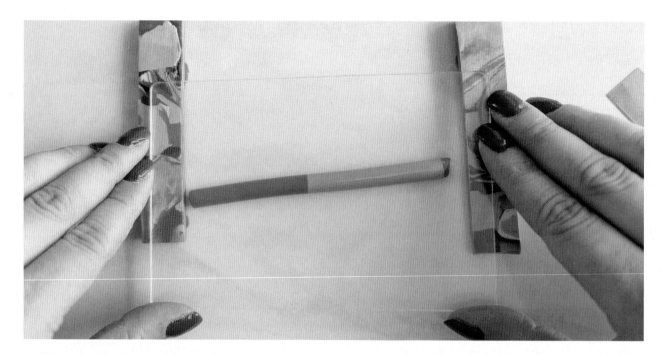

step 8

Place the clay under the acrylic plate once more and roll until it is even and smooth.

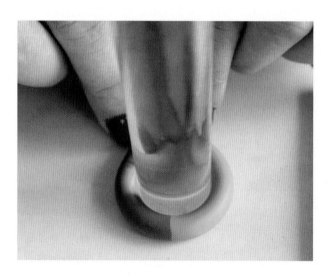

step 9

Once the base color and accent color are even and smooth, the clay is ready to wrap around a mold, such as an acrylic roller. Pinch the ends together and transfer the hoops to the baking sheet. Do not cut the hoops before baking.

Tip » There are commercially available hoop guides you can use to measure your hoops, including silicone hoop guides that can be baked in the oven. You leave the hoops on the silicone hoop guides and just pop them in the oven. The hoop guides shown here are from Goyna Studio.

step 10

Bake the hoops according to the baking guide. Then, while the clay is still warm, cut the ends of the hoops with a precision knife. They are much harder to cut when cool, and you might chip the edges.

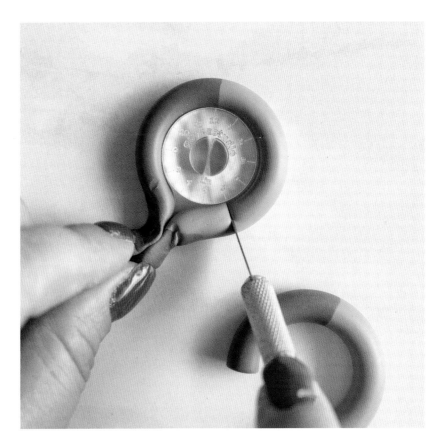

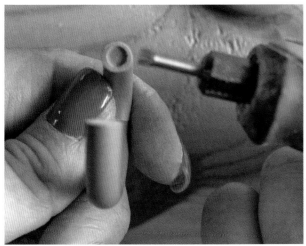

step 11

Once the hoops are cool, mill one end of the hoop with a Dremel with a 3mm flathead drill bit.

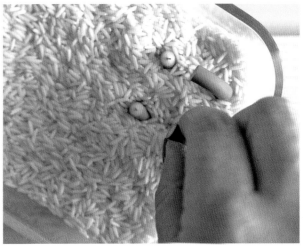

step 12

Fill the milled hole with liquid translucent clay and add a 4mm post. Cover the entire surface with liquid clay by using a toothpick or clay tool. Bake in an oven-safe dish using rice to hold up the hoops.

the ruby

WATERCOLOR METHOD

The watercolor method is a fun and colorful process that's easy to fall in love with. Featuring layers of paint protected by a thin layer of translucent clay, this technique will let your creative side shine.

clay colors & materials

Black: Sculpey Soufflé poppy seed

White: Sculpey Soufflé igloo

Translucent: Sculpey Premo translucent

Acrylic paint in cobalt blue, pale blue, soft pink, and yellow

step 1

For this project, you will need black clay, white clay, and translucent clay. I used Sculpey Soufflé poppyseed, Sculpey Soufflé igloo, and Sculpey Premo translucent. You will also need some acrylic paints; I chose cobalt blue, pale blue, soft pink, and banana yellow. Condition and roll out the black and white clays.

step 2

Lay a piece of white clay on top of a piece of black clay. Cut the pieces to the same size.

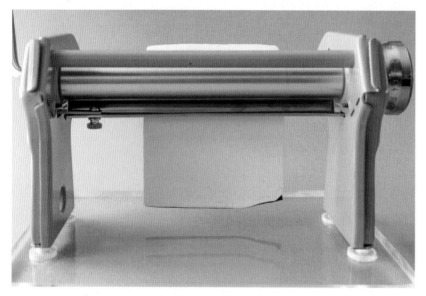

step 3

Roll the doubled-up clay through a pasta machine on the largest setting.

step 4

Turn the pasta machine down two notches; I used the second-to-smallest setting. Roll the clay through it. Do this two or three more times, making a very thin sheet of clay.

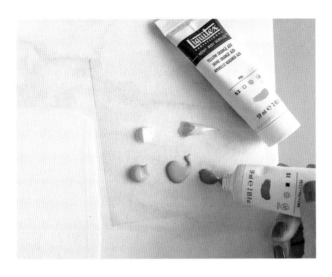

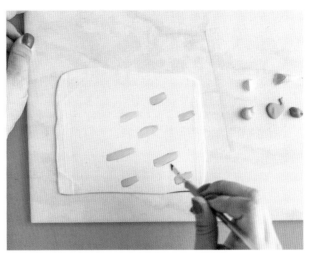

step 5

Dab a dime-sized dollop of each acrylic paint color on your tile or wax paper. Prepare a paintbrush.

step 6

With the white side of the clay facing up, start adding strokes of each color of paint to the slab.

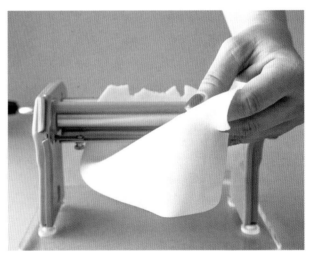

step 7

Make sure the paint is evenly distributed and each color is represented. This can be messy, and it does not have to be perfect. Just have fun! Clean your brush in between each color or use different brushes to avoid mixing colors.

Let the paint dry. It should be fully dry before you proceed to the next step.

step 8

While the paint is drying, condition and roll out the translucent clay. Run the translucent clay through the pasta machine at the largest setting and slowly thin it out to about 1 mm.

step 9

Roll the translucent clay onto the dry, painted slab. Use an acrylic roller to make it smooth and flat.

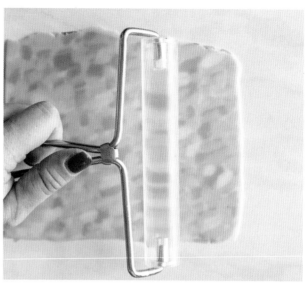

step 10

Pop any bubbles that arise. If air pockets are left in the clay, they will form bubbles in the surface that will remain after baking. Roll over the translucent clay once more, making it smooth and flat.

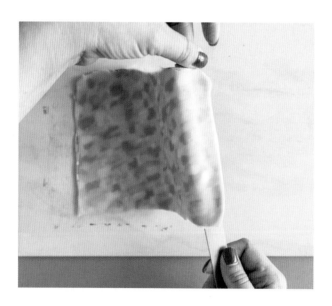

step 11

Remove the translucent clay slab from your tile with a tissue blade. Set it aside.

step 12

Roll out a new piece of white clay for a base. Roll it out about two levels thinner than the largest size on the pasta machine. Rip the painted slab into small pieces and layer it on the base slab.

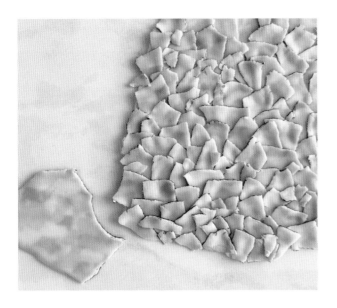

step 13
....

After the base is completely covered in ripped painted pieces, roll the slab with the acrylic roller and run it through the pasta machine on the highest setting.

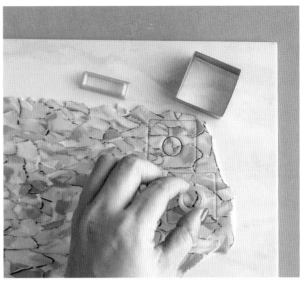

step 14
....

Use clay cutters to make your desired earring shapes. Here I used a square cutter from claytimetools.com.

step 15
....

Remove the excess clay from around the earring shapes and gently remove the earring pieces from the tile with a tissue blade.

Bake the earring pieces according to the baking guide.

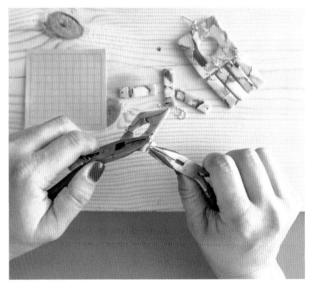

step 16
....

Sand and drill each piece. Add hardware and earring backs to complete the earrings.

pop-art bananas

PAINTING WITH LIQUID CLAY

These adorable bananas will add a fun pop of color to any outfit. Use liquid clay to create the dark spots often seen on ripe bananas.

clay colors & materials

Banana yellow: 3 parts Sculpey Premo yellow and 1 part Sculpey Soufflé canary

Liquid Sculpey clay in black

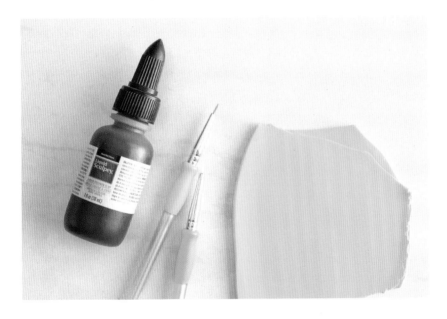

step 1

Condition and roll out the clay using a pasta machine or an acrylic roller.

step 2

Burnish the clay to a tile and cut out banana shapes either with a cutter or with a precision knife and a handmade stencil.

step 3

Remove the excess clay from the slab. Use a tissue blade to remove the raw pieces of clay from the tile and then set them back down on the tile. Removing them before applying paint will help prevent them from warping after they have been painted.

step 4

Squirt a quarter-sized amount of Sculpey liquid clay onto the tile or a piece of wax paper.

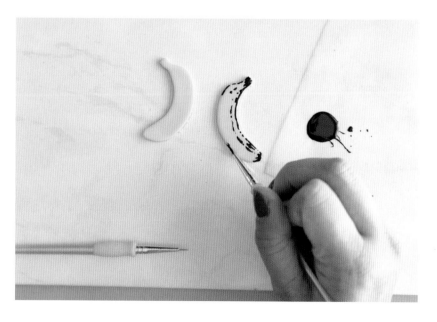

step 5

Use a fine-tip paintbrush to apply your desired design to the bananas.

Pro Tip » Inspired by an iconic piece of artwork? Look for public-domain creative work that has no exclusive intellectual property rights.

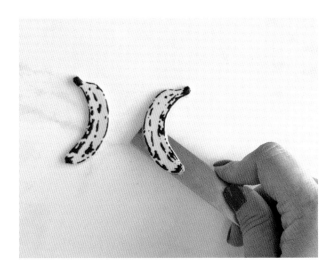

step 6

Transfer the clay pieces to a baking surface. Bake the earring pieces according to the baking guide.

step 7

Sand the earrings so the edges are smooth and clean.

step 8

Drill holes for earring hardware.

step 9

Add hardware and earring backs to complete the earrings.

the sara

GRADIENT AGATE EARRINGS

The agate faux stone method really highlights how versatile polymer clay can be. Rotating thin layers of translucent and colored clay gives the illusion of a sliced agate stone. Use this method to create earrings or the perfect faux stone pendant necklace.

clay colors & materials

Translucent: Sculpey Premo translucent

Pearl: Sculpey Premo pearl

Gray: Sculpey Premo slate

Purple: Sculpey Premo fuchsia

UV resin (hard type)

Gold foil flakes

turning it into a necklace

Any earring project can be made into a pendant necklace. Instead of adding earring posts, simply add a jumpring and put the item on a metal chain, on leather, or on a string. Make a necklace that matches your earrings for a complete look.

step 1

Condition the translucent and fuchsia clays.

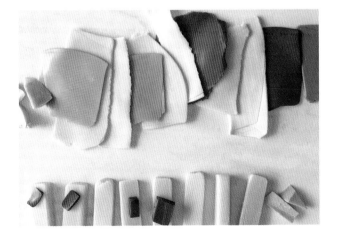

step 2

Cut four pieces of translucent clay. Add a tiny pinch of fuchsia to each of the translucent clay blocks. Mix until you get your desired color. Add a little more to the different blocks until you have four different shades of translucent fuchsia. Keep in mind that the colors will darken in the oven.

Condition and roll out pearl clay and an additional two blocks of translucent clay.

step 3

To make the center of the faux agate, chop up about ⅛ of a block of translucent clay and ⅛ of a block of pearl clay. Using a tissue blade, chop the clays into small pieces, about ⅛ inch each.

step 4

Break up the pieces and try and combine them evenly. Once they are mixed well, push them into a round, pressed log. This will serve as the center of the agate stone.

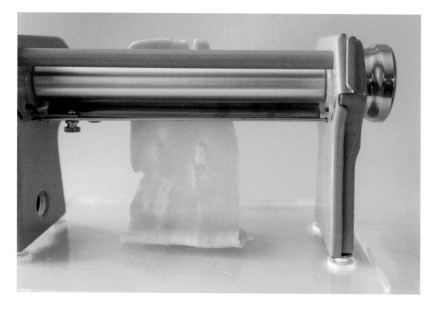

step 5

Condition and thin the colors you previously made in a pasta machine. Gradually change to a lower setting as you thin out the clay. I used the second thinnest setting. Make each color a long, thin strip.

Pro Tip » When recreating something from nature, such as a stone or a flower, research images of the actual thing. Seeing pictures of true agate will help you replicate it.

step 6

Once the strips of clay are laid out, begin to roll each color around the center, one at a time. I chose to start with the lightest fuchsia.

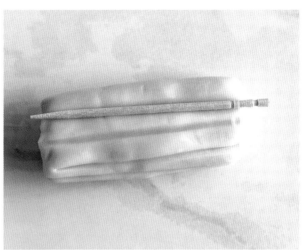

step 7

Use a toothpick, knitting needle, paintbrush, or any long, thin handle to create divots in the sides of the log. Repeat with each layer. This creates the grooves in the agate design.

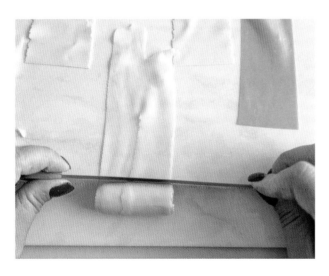

step 8

Between each fuchsia, add a strip of translucent and pearl. You can vary the order of the fuchsia colors.

step 9

Continue layering the thin sheets of clay, rolling them one on top of the other. Pop air bubbles as they arise. I used about 15 layers of clay.

step 10

When you have used all of the fuchsia translucent, plain translucent, and pearl clays, condition the slate color for the outside of the stone. Wrap the slate clay around the log.

step 11

Wrap the clay in a sheet of gold foil. Then roll and condense the log, pushing out any air bubbles.

step 12

Slice the clay log into thin slices and lay them flat on a tile.

Tip » Put the clay in the refrigerator for 30 minutes before cutting it. This will help it firm up for slicing.

step 13

Use a roller to shape the geode slices and burnish them to the tile. Use a toothpick to create large grooves in the sides of the geode. Use the thicker end of a tissue blade to tap the edges to texture the sides of the agate.

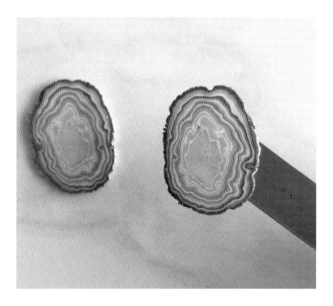

step 14

Bake the earring pieces according to the baking guide. Then sand and drill each piece.

step 15

Add a coat of UV resin (hard type) to create a shiny surface.

Tip » Use a lighter on uncured resin to help raise any bubbles up and out of the surface before curing.

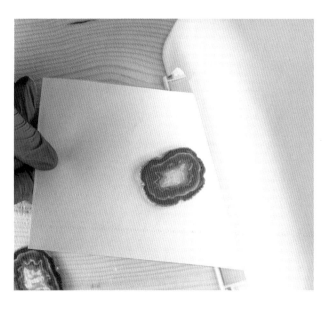

step 16

Cure the resin under a UV lamp.

step 17

Drill the earrings. Add hardware and earring posts to complete the earrings.

baking & after baking

Scrap Clay

So you've made a bunch of earrings, and you have all this extra clay. Now what? Polymer clay is a plastic-based substance, so it is best not to simply toss it in the trash. The good news is, clay doesn't go bad. If properly stored, it can last a long time. In this section, we will talk about getting creative with your scrap clay.

The first tip I can share is to utilize your whole slab. Use every bit of clay surface on your slab to make earrings. Fit as many as possible, and when you can't fit any more, see if you have a small cutter that you can use to make stud earrings.

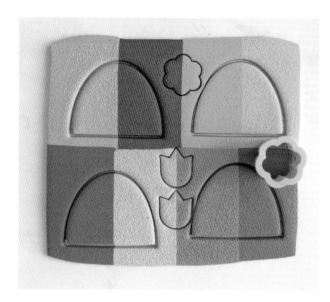

Second, mix your scrap clay into a new color. Make a pile of similar-colored scraps and mix them together. You may be pleasantly surprised! You can also marble your scrap pieces. Use the marbling technique taught in The Rae (pages 62-65) to marble a whole slab or accent pieces.

Making a scrap clay log is another popular way of utilizing scrap clay. Select two or more colors from your scrap clay pile and chop them up into smaller pieces. The smaller the bits, the more intricate the pattern will be. Once the clay is chopped up into small pieces, press it together into a log, working out any air pockets. Slice it, lay it flat, and roll it out into a slab.

Use your scrap clay to get creative. Have a new idea you have been wanting to try? Make a prototype with scrap clay. Use your scrap clay to make photo props like you see in this book. Make an earring stand. Make a tray to hold your tools. Make depth guides like you see in the Maggie (pages 90-95). That is the great thing about polymer clay— you can make anything you can think up!

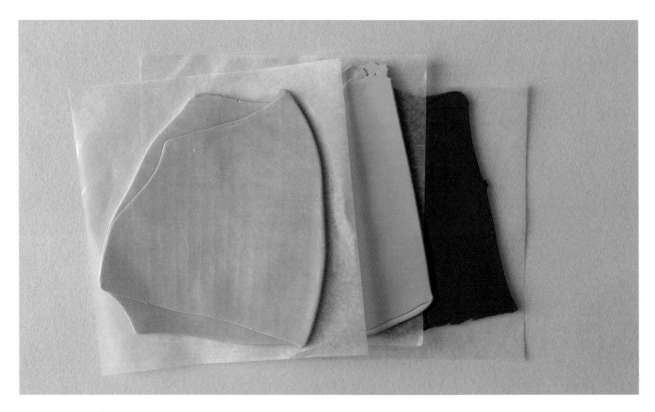

If you are not feeling inspired to use your scrap clay in the moment, be sure to store it properly. I use wax paper to store flat slabs of clay. Purchase patty papers for a quick and easy way to utilize wax paper. You can add flat slabs to a binder with sleeve protectors. To store larger chunks or blocks of clay, you can use glass or plastic bins. Polymer clay can be stored in polypropylene plastic, which can include plastic bags and containers with the recycling symbols with any number between 1 and 5. Polymer clay should be stored properly to keep dust and lint away. It should also be stored out of heat and out of direct sunlight.

Attaching Backs

There are a few different techniques for applying posts to polymer clay in use today. Let's discuss two of the most common and secure options you have for attaching flat back posts to your clay earrings.

Why not just use glue? Attaching posts to your earring backs with glue is an option, but it is not the most secure one. Glue tends to eventually fail. It may last a few months or a few years, but it is not a long-term solution for attaching earring backs. You may find yourself reattaching the earring posts later down the road. If glue is your only option, use a cyanoacrylate adhesive.

Liquid clay method: For more security, you can use liquid clay instead of glue. Place a generous dot of Liquid Sculpey translucent clay on the back of your earring after it is baked. Place the flat back post in the center of the dot and press it in gently. You'll want clay under the post and covering the top of it completely. You may need to use a toothpick or a silicone-tipped clay tool to move the liquid clay around, covering the surface. Bake (yes, bake for a second time, about 20 to 30 minutes at the suggested temperature on the clay packaging) according to the instructions on the liquid clay bottle.

Embedded posts method: Embedding the posts in a thin layer of clay is another secure option. This method leaves a clean, professional-looking back. If you choose this method, you'll need to save extra clay to use after the initial baking and curing process. After the earring has been baked and cooled, add a very small amount of liquid clay to the back of it. Put a flat back post in the center of the liquid clay. Use a toothpick or a silicone-tipped clay tool to spread a very thin layer of liquid polymer clay on the back. Next, roll out a thin layer of polymer clay in the matching color, approximately 1 mm in thickness. Use the same cutter you used for the earring top to cut out matching earring top shapes.

Poke the earring back through the thin piece of clay and gently push the clay down evenly on the back. At this point you'll know if you used too much liquid clay. You can wipe off excess liquid clay with your finger or a baby wipe. Gently smooth the surface of the earring back so it is even and pat down the sides as needed. You can sand any rough edges out from the sides during the sanding process. I have chosen to add texture to the back using sandpaper. This is an optional step. You could instead use a piece of cardstock paper to smooth out the back.

Sanding

Sanding your earring pieces after baking them creates a clean, professional-looking earring. Sanding the front and back of the earring is not necessary, but sanding the sides is highly recommended. You'll notice that after you use clay cutters to cut shapes out of clay, the sides may have ridges, bumps, or excess clay stuck to them. To make the sides smooth, sanding is required.

Safety first: Please note that sanding polymer clay creates a fine dust. To avoid breathing in the fine dust particles, please wear a particle mask. You can also invest in an enclosed sanding station to keep your workstation clear of dust particles.

When you are first starting out, sanding with sandpaper from your local hardware store will do the trick. Start with a lower-grit sandpaper and work your way up to a higher- or finer-grit sandpaper. The lower grit will remove larger grooves or clay bits. The finer-grit sandpaper will help smooth out the surface. I usually start with 150 grit and move my way to 500 grit and then to 1000 grit, depending on how soft the clay is and how smooth the edges are. Different clay cutters and clay brands will require different levels of sanding.

If you plan on making a lot of earrings, I recommend investing in a Dremel. A Dremel is a rotary tool that can make sanding and drilling easier and faster. Use soft felt tip attachments to sand the edges with ease. The felt tips come in different shapes and sizes.

Use a nail file to sand those hard-to-reach grooves or corners in your earrings.

Here is a before-and-after shot to show you what a difference sanding makes!

Texture

Let's get creative with texture! Having a smooth, clean finish for an earring surface is a wonderful thing. It works for many designs. Adding texture can give an extra element to a pair of earrings. Texture can be subtle, or it can steal the show. Here is how to achieve various textures using clay-specific tools and items you can find in your home.

You can purchase tools specifically designed for polymer clay that add fun texture to your earring designs. You can even create your own! Many shops will create custom texture mats or sheets based on your own designs for something truly unique.

Sandpaper, toothbrush & foil

You don't need to invest a ton of money to achieve texture. You can use everyday items from around your house to give your earrings a unique look. In this book, you have seen sandpaper used multiple times to create a textured surface. This look can also be attained by a toothbrush, foil, or a scrubber brush. Please keep in mind that polymer clay is nontoxic but not considered food safe. Once an item has been used on raw clay, it should not be used on food, even if it's been run through the dishwasher.

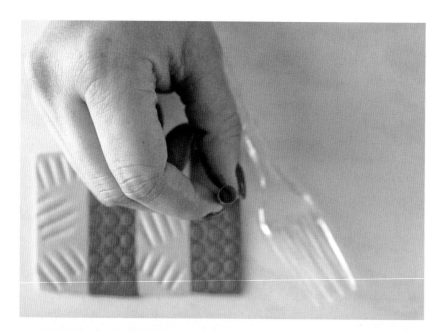

Fork & straw

Raid the utensil drawer! Use a plastic fork to create lines in your clay. Cut a straw down and use it to create circles in the surface of your clay. Get inventive! Is there something in your home with a cool texture or surface print? Give it a try!

Cutters

Clay cutters can double as stamps. On this clay slab, I used the micro floral cutter to cut out red flowers and added them to the surface. I rolled the slab flat and then used the same cutter to stamp each red flower and added other floral stamps to give the clay surface a little more depth and detail.

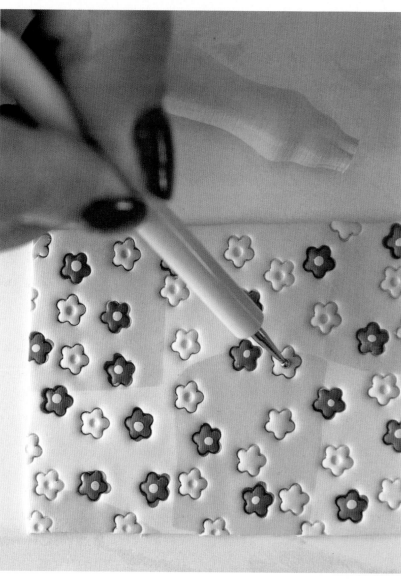

Baking Guide

Baking is a critical part of the earring-making process. It can also be one of the most frustrating parts. Polymer clay is hardened only through baking. You do not need an expensive kiln to bake it; you can use your kitchen oven or a tabletop oven. Because it is a plastic-based substance, polymer clay is meant to be flexible and durable. If it is not cured properly, it will be brittle and break easily. And spending hours and hours creating something only to have it break can be heartbreaking. So, let's go over some key elements to ensure your success during the baking process.

Before baking your clay, prepare a clean surface for your earring pieces. You can use a ceramic surface for baking (e.g., a ceramic tile), a metal baking sheet, or even a piece of cardboard. I recommend placing a piece of copy paper or cardstock paper in between your clay pieces and your baking surface. The paper or cardboard will not burn at low temperatures, and it will help create a smooth, clean earring back. If your earrings are baked directly on a shiny surface, it can leave splotchy marks on the back.

Let your oven preheat fully before inserting your tray of earring pieces. Ovens spike in temperature while preheating. If you put your earrings in before the preheating process is complete, you run the risk of messing up the curing process.

The most important tool for baking is your oven. You are probably thinking that is a no-brainer, but let me explain. Your oven needs to hold consistent, accurate temperature for the appropriate amount of time for the polymer clay to cure properly. Curing is the bonding of the clay's chemical structure, making it flexible and durable.

There are essentially two reasons why polymer clay might not cure properly. The first is that the oven is not the right temperature. The second is the length of time that the polymer clay is baked. Most clay package instructions give you a certain time and temperature at which to bake, but you may need to play around to get it right.

If your polymer clay is burning, your oven is too hot. Some ovens run hot, and if yours runs even 10 degrees hotter than it says it does, it will mess up the curing process. Investing in an oven thermometer and testing the accuracy of your oven is a simple fix to this issue. If your oven fluctuates and does not maintain a consistent temperature, your clay will not cure and will be brittle, no matter how long you bake it. Keeping an eye on your oven thermometer during the baking process will tell you if your oven fluctuates in temperature.

Most polymer clay baking instructions say to bake the clay for 15 minutes per ¼ inch, about 30 minutes for your average tray of earrings. I recommend baking a little longer. I bake my earrings for 45 to 60 minutes.

Earrings may vary in thickness from beads to large statement earrings to small studs. In addition, each clay maker will have a personal preference regarding how thick their earrings are made. Use your scrap clay to test baking times and temperatures. Make scrap pieces in various thicknesses and bake them at different time intervals. Let them cool fully before testing their flexibility and durability.

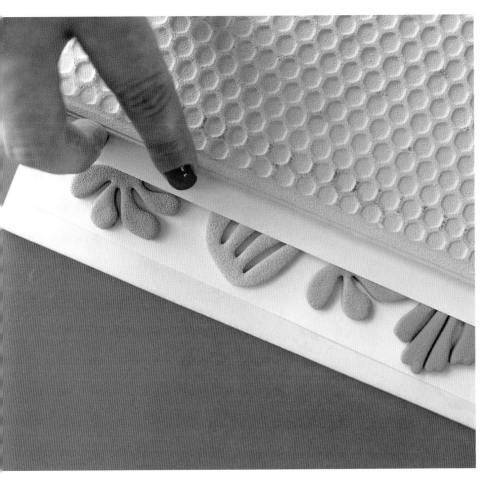

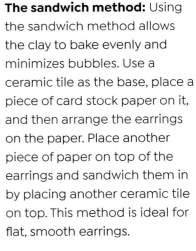

The sandwich method: Using the sandwich method allows the clay to bake evenly and minimizes bubbles. Use a ceramic tile as the base, place a piece of card stock paper on it, and then arrange the earrings on the paper. Place another piece of paper on top of the earrings and sandwich them in by placing another ceramic tile on top. This method is ideal for flat, smooth earrings.

The tent method: If the sandwich method does not work for your earring design—for example, if they have texture or a raised design—the tent method is a great option. Use a piece of foil or a disposable aluminum baking dish to cover your earring pieces, or make a "tent" over them. This allows for even airflow and baking.

These methods are by no means necessary, but if you are having baking issues or issues with bubbles surfacing during the baking process, it is worth exploring them.

The baking process is worth investing your time in. You may have no issues at all, but if anything does come up, I hope this guide will help you troubleshoot any issues. Having properly cured earring pieces makes all the difference in the world.

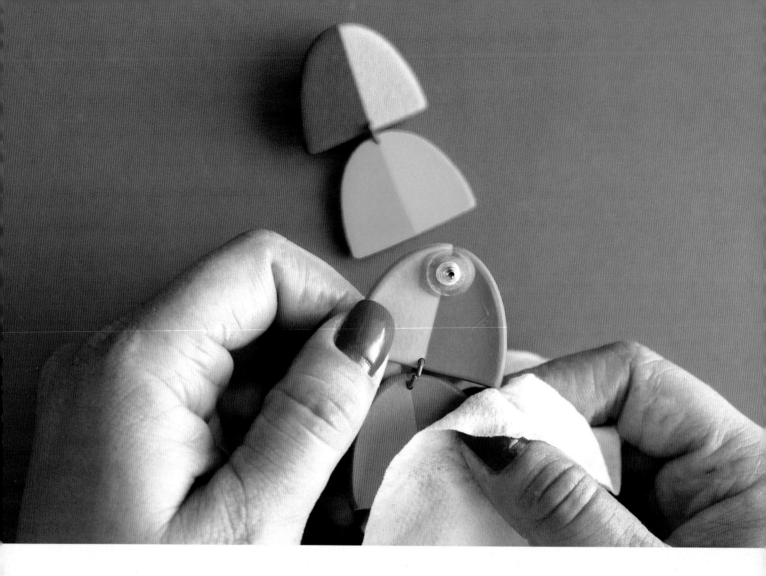

Cleaning & Care

Although polymer clay jewelry is durable and flexible, don't bend it intentionally or harshly. It should be stored hanging or laid flat. Polymer clay is water resistant, but it's best not to wear polymer jewelry in the water to avoid discoloration of the jewelry findings.

If your polymer clay earrings get dirty—for example, if they get makeup on them—simply wash them with soap and water or with a baby wipe. If you have stubborn stains on your polymer clay jewelry, you can clean them with acetone on a cotton swab. Acetone can discolor darker clays, so this is only recommended for lighter clay earrings with stubborn stains.

about the author

Rachael Skidmore is a self-taught polymer clay artist based out of Salt Lake City, Utah. Her passion for self-expression, penchant for artistic creativity, and dedication to hard work have been the foundation of her success as the small business owner of **Made by Maeberry** for more than 10 years.

While she is widely recognized in the polymer clay community for producing high-quality pieces, her voice of genuine support for inclusivity is what makes her stand out as a creator. A curator of color with a knack for original design and tantalizing patterns, Rachael takes inspiration from all aspects of her life, from her passion for vintage clothing to her love for hiking in the mountains with her family.

Rachael has inspired large audiences through her social media presence online and delivers hands-on teaching by hosting intimate classes in person.

In 2021, through Domestika, she launched an online course on polymer clay basics. Now with this book, Rachael is thrilled to provide that same intimate setting to deliver high-quality instruction to artists all over the world.